The Pan Am Journey

BOB, ENJOY THE TRIP.

Tom Kewin

The Pan Am Journey

THOMAS KEWIN

To order additional copies of this book, contact:
Xlibris Corporation
1-888-795-4274
www.Xlibris.com
Orders@Xlibris.com
28047

Contents

Acknowledgements 7

Clipper To Hawaii 9
Youthful Dreams 15
Training 19
Aircraft 24
    Martin M-130 24
    Boeing B314a 26
    Consolidated Pb2y3r 30
    Martin Pbm3r 31
Pacific Stations 34
    Pearl Harbor 34
    Palmyra Island 36
    Canton Island 36
    Wallis Island 37
    Suva 38
    Auckland 38
    Brisbane 40
    Funafuti 40
    Noumea 41
    Espiritu Santos 42
Line Operations 43
    Board And Lodgings 43
    Moana Hotel 45
    Aircraft Maintenance 46
    Casting Off 49
    Crew Protocol 50
    Take-off Problems 52
    Cruising 53
    The Experience 55
Genius 57

Post War 60
Military Service 65
Douglas Dc–4 69
Peaceful Pacific 72
　　Wake Island 74
　　Midway 77
　　Guam 78
　　Manila 79
　　Fiji 81
　　Hong Kong.. 82
　　Shanghai 85
　　Bangkok.. 86
　　Calcutta 88
The Experiment 89
Stewardesses 93
Delhi Belly 97
Stratocruiser 101
Atlantic Division 107
Lockheed Constellation 109
Rainbow Class 114
Home Again 120
More Stewardesses 125
Jets 128
Jumbo 141
Roswell.. 144
Teething Problems 151
Jumbo Tales 153
　　Malaysia 153
　　Passengers 156
Flight 845 To Tokyo 161
Storm Clouds 166
Hope Parkinson Kewin 171
Phyllis.. 173

Final Note.. 177

ACKNOWLEDGEMENTS

Jane Gottschall, author of "As Pistons Flew", has been the goad that kept me writing, and writing, and rewriting. Her editing skills and personal Pan Am experience were very helpful.

R.E.G. Davies, noted aviation author and publisher, encouraged my early efforts. As an authority on Pan American history, and many other things, he is a delightful advisor. I treasure his lessons on the English language with a capital "E".

CLIPPER TO HAWAII

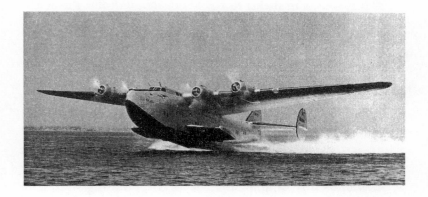

Boeing 314

Captain Smith was not just an airline Captain; he was a "Master of Ocean Flying", with a certificate signed by Pan American Vice President Andre Priester. Before coming to Pan American in the mid 1930s he had graduated from college, earned his Navy wings at Pensacola, and served four years Naval service. In addition to the normal pilot certificates, he also held an Air Transport Rating, Aircraft and Engine Mechanic certificate, a Second Class Radio license, and was qualified as a Navigator. He had taken many company courses, including international law, company history, and meteorology. On this August afternoon of 1940

he made the take-off in the *Honolulu Clipper* flying boat from
San Francisco Bay and climbed the airplane over the Golden
Gate Bridge toward Hawaii, 2,100 miles away.

With an estimated flying time of more than 16 hours, a
large crew was necessary to allow some rest periods. There
were four pilots, a navigator, two engineers, two radio
operators, and two stewards, making a total of eleven
crewmembers. On the flight segment from San Francisco to
Honolulu, because of the limited payload to ensure adequate
fuel, the crew usually outnumbered the passengers.

The usual summer fog bank that cooled San Francisco
had retreated to the ocean side of the San Francisco-Oakland
bay bridge, leaving a few white patches on the hills to the
north and south and providing a fair west wind and slightly
choppy water in the bay.

Mrs. Smith watched the take-off from their home in the
Berkeley Hills. She could not always see the airplane, but
the white wake was a clearly visible line across the water, and
when it disappeared she knew he was airborne. As the
airplane flew over the bridge and fog and on towards the
setting sun everything seemed to be functioning well. The
indicated airspeed matched the performance charts, as well
as the Flight Time Analysis provided by the Pan American
Dispatch Office. The westward progress seemed to slow the
world a bit so they enjoyed a lengthy sunset. When the sky
darkened the pilots deployed the folded curtains behind
the cockpit and prepared for a long night. Two hours later,
Captain Smith allowed the Third Officer to relieve him and
went downstairs for dinner. He chatted with the passengers
as they were enjoying their cocktails, and joined three of
them for dinner at a table in the main lounge. A white
tablecloth covered the dining table, and dinner was served
on special Pan American china with custom silver utensils
and crystal. Soup was followed by a main course of roast beef,
mashed potatoes, asparagus, and a green salad. When the
table was cleared, coffee and an ice cream dessert were

served. The Captain declined the coffee and after-dinner drinks, and retired to the forward (A) compartment, where he took off his uniform and slid into the freshly made bunk for a two-hour nap. When the Purser awakened him he dressed, refreshed himself, and chatted for a few minutes in the galley, while drinking a cup of black coffee. The cabin was dark and quiet, as most of the passengers had retired to their berths, and the quiet rumble of the engines and gentle movement of the aircraft had put most of them immediately to sleep. Smith climbed the circular stairs to the dimly-lit flight deck and stopped at the Flight Radio Operator's desk.

He knew that the Radio Operator was probably listening to the baseball game on station KPO so he asked; "How are the Seals doing, 'Cush?"

"Doing good, skipper. They are up 6 to 4 over the Oaks. O'Doul has two hits and a stolen base."

"Good, let me know how it comes out". Then he took a few steps aft to the Flight Engineer's station.

"Everything all right, Jim?"

"Yes sir, the Howgozit is on track, and we have gained 8 minutes on the flight plan. That number 2 engine has a sticking exhaust valve, so I am running the cylinder heads 10 degrees cool, but it may bark once in a while if that valve hangs open. Number 4 is still burning some oil, but I just transferred 4 gallons to the tank".

Now the Captain moved across to the large Navigator's table for a few words, then waited as he finished some calculations.

"Are the winds behaving, Magellan?"

The Navigator pulled out the wind chart, and pointing to a circular set of lines said;

"I think that low pressure area is much further north than forecast, so we are getting lighter headwinds than expected. I am just now doing calculations for a three-star fix, which I will start shooting in 8 minutes."

Smith answered; "Good, when you are ready to start, let me know and I will hand-fly it."

On automatic pilot the airplane developed a very slight rolling motion, which was not noticeable to the passengers but was very obvious to the Navigator. With the octant glued to his eye while trying to keep the star target and a bubble level in central focus, the slight movement of the airplane was very trying. Because of this uncertainty, the star shot was always taken three times and then averaged out.

Now Captain Smith stepped through the lightproof curtains into the cockpit to start the shift change. The young Third Officer relinquished the Captain's left hand seat and Smith strapped himself into it. He settled into his comfortable command post slowly, carefully adjusted the seat position, put on his leather gloves, and tried his grip on the control wheel. The First Officer, on his right, briefed Smith on altitude, heading, and control trim settings, and then went below for his rest period, allowing the Third Officer (relief pilot) to replace him. After a careful scan of the flight instruments and the sky ahead, the Captain called for an engine inspection. The Third Officer retrieved the Aldis lamp, a high-powered hand-held lantern, and made a visual examination of the front of numbers 3 and 4 engines, then handed the lamp to the Captain, who made a similar scan of numbers 1 and 2 engines. Smith disengaged the autopilot to check the aircraft trim settings, and be ready for the Navigator's star shot. As fuel is consumed, the lower weight of the aircraft changes the flight dynamics and the airplane flies a little differently, so the trim controls must be adjusted to maintain minimum aerodynamic drag. With the star shot complete, he engaged the autopilot, checked the magnetic heading, and the *Honolulu Clipper* droned on westward through the night.

The Navigator averaged the elevations, the upward angles of the three stars he aimed at, and when they were plotted on the large navigation chart, they described a triangle.

Somewhere in the middle of that triangle was the probable location of the airplane at that moment.

In the meantime, the relief Engineer had awakened. Most of the Engineers preferred a cooler environment for their rest area, so had installed a single cot in the center wing section. It was noisier, but had better air circulation and most slept well there. Before sitting down at the desk, the fresh Engineer crawled out through the wing tunnels to inspect the back of all four engines, and the fuel and oil lines in the leading edge of the wing, then sat for a few minutes of briefing from the other Engineer. In a similar manner the two Radio Operators were keeping a four-hour watch schedule, the Stewards were taking rest turns, and one of the navigation-qualified pilots gave the Navigator a rest period.

The "Still Air" flying time between San Francisco and Honolulu was 16 hours and 12 minutes, but the prevailing westerly winds could readily increase that by two hours, or more. Weather forecasting was still a very inexact science so adequate fuel reserves were carried, and the crew kept a watchful eye on forward progress and fuel consumption. The "Howgozit" chart was a graphic presentation of the flights status, reflecting fuel consumption and miles traveled compared to the Dispatcher's forecast. A glance at the chart could tell you more in ten seconds than five minutes of looking at numbers. On some occasions, especially during winter months, radical changes in the weather could result in the airplane falling so far behind that it was necessary to turn around and return to San Francisco.

A few hours after sunrise the passengers and crew enjoyed a full breakfast, and preparations began for arrival in Honolulu. Captain Smith shaved and put on a fresh shirt, as did the rest of the crew. With the mountain peaks of Hawaii in sight, the throttles were brought back to idle and the aircraft started a quiet descent around the Diamond Head landmark. At minimum power, the aircraft swept past

Waikiki, downtown Honolulu and the Aloha Tower, and made a gentle turn into the mouth of Pearl Harbor. Almost magically the airplane settled back to the water, and quickly slowed as it sank deeper into the harbor. As the Clipper taxied toward the Pearl City terminal, the passengers stirred in preparation to disembark, and then stood and waited. It took a while for the docking crew to attach the "Pelican Hook" to the rear of the airplane, the bow line to a buoy, and maneuver the airplane backwards to the dock in front of the terminal. When all was secured, the passengers disembarked and walked up the ramp to the small terminal, wearing the leis heaped on them by the PAA ground staff. The crew assembled on the dock, where the First Officer handed the ship's papers to a representative from Operations, the Engineers handed the maintenance logbook to the chief mechanic, and the crew marched in formation, two by two, in naval fashion into the terminal building.

YOUTHFUL DREAMS

Young Tom

In August 1940, accompanied by two friends, I drove to Treasure Island in San Francisco Bay to spend another day at the great World Fair. From our home in Modesto, California, it was about a two-hour drive in my 1929 Ford Roadster, but with an early start we arrived as the gates opened. The Billy Rose Aquacade, Sally Rand and her fans, the General Electric "House of the Future" and all the other attractions were great, but my focus was on the Pan American Airways hangar. There was a walkway above the hangar floor open to visitors when one of the Clippers was in the hangar. I spent hours watching dozens of mechanics service the airplane. A full day at the Fair was mind-boggling to an 18 year-old college student, but that Clipper-Ship lying at the dock on the lagoon was, if not out of this world, out of mine.

On this visit we were lucky, and had the chance to watch the dramatic departure. As we pressed against the fence we heard one bell sound, and the entire crew came marching out of the lower level of the Terminal Building. A short time later two bells sounded, and the passengers were escorted to the airplane. The men wore suits, ties, and hats, and the ladies were in high heels, gloves, and furs, quite a contrast to the casual attire today. Soon the four engines roared to life, the lines were cast off, and the Clipper glided gracefully into the Bay. We watched as full power was applied and the giant ship thundered across the water and finally lifted off toward the Golden Gate. I thought about that Clipper crew flying to Hawaii as I "flew" that old Ford down the highway to home. I knew that I wanted to do something in aviation, but my eyes would not meet the 20-20 requirements of a pilot, so I settled on an Aeronautical Engineer objective. I had never heard of a "Flight Engineer".

The position of "Flight Engineer" was developed at Pan American Airways to meet the needs of advancing technology. Today, Flight Engineers have disappeared because of advancing technology. The latest model of the Boeing 747-400 is a marvel of automation and two pilots can easily handle all operating functions. The aircraft has built-in troubleshooting features and automatic system controls so that a Flight Engineer is no longer needed. The aircraft factories will never again build an airliner with an Engineers station. I was fortunate to be in the right place at the right time.

Flight Engineers were originally drawn from the maintenance shops, but by 1939 the airline had started a more demanding program to train future engineers. An

Aeronautical Engineering degree was the first requirement, plus at least two years in the maintenance shops. An Aircraft and Engine Mechanics license was required (in later years, with the advent of Jets, the Engine Mechanics license was changed to read "Power Plant Mechanic". Six months as Chief Mechanic at an overseas station was desirable. When a vacancy occurred the applicant started training. This was all well and good, given the slow and orderly growth of the airline, but the Second World War changed the program considerably. With military contracts demanding rapid expansion there was no time for lengthy training programs, and the Maintenance Department needed every qualified mechanic it had, and more. Flight Engineer "Jocko" Parrish was sent on a recruiting trip. He hired young engineering graduates at Purdue, Chicago, Colorado, and other engineering schools, telling them to report to Treasure Island for training. Some were aeronautical engineers, some were mechanical engineers, and two were even mining engineers. And some, like me, were in between. I walked in off the street. After two years of Civil Engineering studies at Modesto Junior College, I had been accepted at Stanford. Because of the war, and my interest in airplanes, I went instead to the Boeing School of Aeronautics (owned by United Air Lines) at Oakland Airport to obtain an Aeronautical Engineering degree in 18 months. The school charged a tuition fee of $100 a month, and living costs would be another $100, which put it beyond what my father could afford. I talked to my grandmother about what I wanted to do, and she said she would send me a check for $200 every month. Before I could finish the course the Army Air Corps took over the school to train mechanics; but United Air Lines offered me a job as a Flight Engineer on the B-24s (C-87s) it was to operate for the Air Transport Command. After a month of training I was sent to the maintenance shops to work as a mechanic while waiting for a crew assignment.

We heard that Pan American was hiring Flight Engineers, so on a Thursday my two housemates, Fitch Robertson and Charles Emery, went to Treasure Island and were hired to start training on the next Monday. I rushed to Treasure Island the next day, Friday, and was told by "Spec" Winchester in the personnel office that he had just hired two engineers and did not need any more. He said that he would keep my application on file, but I knew what file that would likely be (the circular one), so I went upstairs and found the Chief Flight Engineer's office. Carl "Cocky" Green was very pleasant, and we had a nice half-hour chat. Then he called downstairs and told "Spec" to put me on the payroll on Monday at $138 per month! United was paying me $350 but I didn't care. The *China Clipper* at last! In later years Carl told me that he was not eager to hire a green 20-year-old, but he had a class starting and needed one more body. And, he figured he could always fire me.

Someone in the military high command had the good sense to preserve Pan Am throughout the war, and to make use of its expertise in over-ocean flying. All critical personnel were inducted into the Navy, and placed on "inactive duty". That meant that we were beyond the reach of the draft board, as long as we stayed with the airline. A further reason was that we would be operating Naval Aircraft, and civilians could not do that. Should the Japanese forces capture us, as military personnel we could hope to be treated according to the rules of the Geneva Convention. As civilians we would be executed as spies.

TRAINING

Ground school at Treasure Island was six days a week, eight to five, and it went on for five months. We had to qualify on four aircraft; The Martin M-130 (China Clipper), The Boeing B314, The Consolidated PB2Y3R (Coronado), and the Martin PBM3A (Mariner). As the airline was on a cost-plus 6% contract we were given the best training available, and it was superb. They even brought in Professor Metz from Cal Poly to teach a one-week course on the care and feeding of large, round, aircraft power plants. The last day of the class was devoted to engine operating procedures, trouble-shooting, and economical engine operation. Sixty years later, the phrase "Stoichiometrically correct fuel-air ratio" still makes my stomach churn!

Training flights were assigned when available. My first flight on the Boeing 314 was on a "slow time" 12-hour flight with Captain Steve Bancroft. When an airplane came out of overhaul it was sent on a long "shakedown" flight before being put back into service. With four newly overhauled engines this was probably a good idea. There were so many students and observers on board that they even put on two stewards to prepare our meals. It was an ideal first exposure, because we students had ample time to explore the wing tunnels and nacelles, sit at the Engineers Station for a few hours, and even take a nap. Captain Bancroft had his own agenda. After flying over Mount Shasta, Lake Tahoe, and

Yosemite National Park he headed for Fresno, his hometown. He put down some wing flaps, descended to about 400 feet, and while the copilot flew some left circles over a friend's ranch house, Steve took rocks from his briefcase and pelted the barn through his sliding window.

Ground school was intensive, with many instructors from all parts of the airline. Most of them were Flight Engineers, including Eddie Abarr, Russ Goodson, and Hugh Cone, but there were some professional instructors as well. One of them who sticks in my mind was a retired Navy Chief Petty Officer named "Sales", who taught us about emergency equipment and seamanship. He was so knowledgeable and enthusiastic about his subject that he managed to arouse some of that feeling in his class of young landlubbers. I can still tie a "bowline knot" with my hands behind my back, and "lay a bowline on a bight". He also taught us the specific uses of each knot, and I still benefit from the instruction. (It was helpful during my five-year stint as a scoutmaster.)

The traditional role of the Flight Engineer was that of an onboard mechanic and troubleshooter, but now we were also expected to be the experts on "Cruise Control", and "Howgozits". For days we struggled to understand those complex charts that the engine manufacturers produced to define Horsepower with RPM, Manifold Pressure, Fuel Flow, Temperature' and Altitude, all of them twisted together on a graphic chart. It took a long time for us to finally grasp the significance of each variable. The classes on aerodynamics were limited to discussions about our specific aircraft. I remember Russ Goodson explaining the theory of "wing-washing". Upon leveling at the selected altitude the pilot accelerated to a speed slightly above the planned cruise speed. In theory this higher speed would "wash" off some of the inherent drag from the wing surface and, as the aircraft settled produce a slightly higher airspeed. An alternative technique was to climb a few hundred feet higher than the desired altitude and "dive" back down. As one of our most valuable contributions was to be "trouble-shooting", we were expected to learn every aircraft system. We might be asked to draw a schematic of the generator-charging system from memory, or describe the proper way to adjust the idle-mixture strength on the engine.

Once a month a seminar was held to discuss on-line problems, and we were encouraged to sit in. Twenty or thirty Engineers would sit down for the day and talk about their latest trips, and the problems they had. For us students it was a very valuable session, as we began to get some idea of the task ahead of us. I remember Bill Lincoln talking about the problems with the "Jack and Heintz" starters on the PB2Y3s. On his recent trip to Espiritu Santos the engage solenoids had failed on two of the engine starters and no spares were available. The starters had a "manual engage" lever, but on a seaplane it was awkward to use. Bill strung long lengths of heavy stainless steel "safety wire" from the engage levers at the engines to the top fuselage hatch. When he had the starter motor up to speed, he gave the signal to the other Engineer who pulled on the wire and the starter worked. He coaxed the airplane all the way home with those wires flapping in the slipstream. "Jocko" Parrish talked about the cracks in the PBM exhaust stacks. Russ Goodson explained a new technique for "internally air cooling" the engines on the *Coronados* by operating at full throttle with the mixture control leaned to provide only enough fuel for the desired power. It was a complicated procedure that I did not understand until I tried it six months later. (And used to good effect on the Lockheed Constellation) These seminars were a valuable part of our training, and were typical of the all out effort the group was making to operate efficiently. Down the hall, similar training was going on for newly hired-pilots, radio operators, and navigators. The navigators were frequently on the roof taking "Sun Shots" with their octants, and we were all sharing life rafts during emergency training in the "Clipper Lagoon".

In the beginning I felt I was in over my head. All these people seemed to know so much, and I so little, but as it went on I was gaining confidence and knowledge. By the time I was able to give some tutoring to a few of the newer hires I knew I would be all right.

Training flights were always a mass movement of people, and sometimes memorable. On a breezy and cold Easter morning we started take-off in a PB2Y3 from San Pablo Bay. In the rough water, as the airplane just started to rise up on the "step", it began to "porpoise", pitching up and down. With every downward pitch the seawater washed over the windshield, and some of it briefly choked the engines. Captain Beer, the instructor, closed the throttles, forgetting that he had already ordered the student co-pilot to punch the button to retract the wingtip floats. As the airplane lost forward speed it settled on the right side, with the No.4, or right outside propeller splashing water, so I shut that engine down. We tried to extend the wing tip floats, but the electric motor stalled when it tried to lift the wing out of the water. Captain Beer reasoned that if he could get enough forward speed he could get the airplane "planing" on the "step" and could then extend the tip floats. It did not work, as the more power he applied to the inboard engines the deeper the wing tip float dug into the water. Finally, on that chilly morning, I was sent out to the "down" wing and, working in a foot of sea water, took off an access panel and disconnected the drive mechanism to that tip float. Then we electrically drove down the float on the opposite wing. With "all hands on deck" on the high wing the airplane slowly settled to the extended tip float, and we taxied slowly back to the Treasure Island base.

During this period of intensive training a few of my fellow students disappeared when they were found to be lacking in aptitude for the job, and a few chose to try something else. The training was like a merry-go-round. You got on, and when you had completed the circuit, you grabbed the brass ring and got off. The brass ring entitled you to six months on the shores of Pearl Harbor.

I arrived at the Pearl City base a few months after my twenty first birthday, but I was feeling much older.

AIRCRAFT

MARTIN M-130

Martin 130

Delivered to Pan American in 1935, the three M130s (at a cost of $417,000 each) were the aircraft that launched scheduled service across the Pacific Ocean. The earlier flights with the Sikorsky S-42 were for survey and proving purposes only. They did not have the ability to carry a useful load on the long flight from San Francisco to Honolulu, and even the M-130 was marginal. The Martin's advertised cruising speed of 157 mph was never realized in service. Using the Long Range Cruising technique a more realistic speed was around 125 mph. I made my first productive flight to

Honolulu on the *China Clipper* in September, 1943, and it took more than 22 hours. (A few months later the airplane was sent to Miami). The Flight Engineers station was in the pylon that connected the wing to the fuselage, up a catwalk to the rear of the cockpit. A small window on each side gave a view of the bottom of the wings and the engines. Instrument panels and engine controls were scattered about and the seat was mounted against the main wing spar. The vibration and noise were unbelievable, which may help account for the hearing aids I wear. In that environment interphone headsets were impractical, so a "telegraph system" was installed. It consisted of a lever at the Pilot station connected to a lever at the Engineer station. When the Pilot wanted the Engineer to start engines he moved the lever to the "Start Engines" position, but the connecting cables were so long that the indication at the Engineer's end might be something else. By flipping it back and forth the Pilot could gain the engineer's attention well enough to give him hand signals of what he wanted. Sitting at the Engineer's station, to my left were two five-gallon, glass water separators through which all the fuel flowed, and I sometimes thought about the consequences of a crash—fifteen difficult feet from the nearest exit and likely to be doused in gasoline. The very reliable Pratt & Whitney Twin Wasp engines delivered 900 horsepower to the Hamilton Standard Constant-Speed propellers. In 1940 those propellers were replaced by the latest full-feathering models.

Glenn Martin had made a calculated gamble when he agreed to build the M-130 for Pan American. He knew that the contracted price would not fully cover the development costs, but expected follow-on orders to make up for it. And he was determined to build the airplane. With an empty weight of 25,400 lbs and a maximum weight of 52,000 lbs it was a phenomenal airplane, in that it could lift over twice its own weight. I do not know of any other transport aircraft that could do that. When Pan Am's founder, Juan Trippe, asked the manufacturers for a bigger airplane Martin came up with a larger version of the M-130 called the M-156, but Boeings B-314 design was selected. The Martin airplane was sold to the Soviet Union as the *Russian Clipper,* and was flown in the Russian Far East for two years.

The *Hawaii Clipper* disappeared between Guam and Manila in 1938, probably flew into a violent storm. The *Philipine Clipper* hit a mountain 100 miles north of San Francisco in 1943, six weeks before I was hired. The *China Clipper* crashed at Port of Spain, Trinidad early in 1945. When this last of the Martin Clippers crashed, it had flown more than 20,000 hours.

BOEING B314A

Flight Engineer Station, Boeing 314

The big Boeing was one of the most beautiful airplanes ever built, but unfortunately all twelve of them are gone.

The airplane was a symbol of pride to the employees and to all Americans. The late-afternoon departure of the Clipper for Honolulu invariably drew a crowd of onlookers as the crew marched aboard and the engines were started. Many of the onlookers, including me, were employees whose work shift had ended an hour earlier, but stayed on to watch the dramatic lift-off. As the aircraft finally cleared the surface, with water streaming from the hull, it was a glorious sight. On into the afternoon sunlight and over the coastal fog bank the Clipper was an artist's dream. We used to say that the low wages were compensated by the glory of working on the Clippers, and we were not joking.

At a cost of more than a million dollars each (with spares) the aircraft represented a huge investment, on which the primary return was not to be from passengers, but from a subsidy in the form of mail payments. (at a rate of $2.00 a mile). President Juan Trippe had vast plans for these new giants of the sky; not only to cross the Pacific Ocean, but the Atlantic as well, but there was a political snag. The British did not have an aircraft that could profitably cross the Atlantic and they did not want to give Pan American permission to fly to England until they were in a position to fly to the U.S.A. The logical solution was to sell three of the Boeings to the British, and that is what they did. While the sale was being consummated and delivery made, England was plunged into war and all thoughts of flying the Atlantic were forgotten. Instead, the renamed "Speedbirds" were put to productive use maintaining a lifeline to the military forces and diplomatic staff in Africa.

The remaining nine aircraft became the backbone of the Pan American fleet. The flight deck was huge, over nineteen feet long and ten feet wide, with full headroom. The pilot stations could be curtained off at night, allowing the rest of the flight deck to be well illuminated. At the rear of the flight deck a small door on either side gave access to the tunnels inside the wings, which led to the back of all four engines. Aft of the flight deck, through another door, was a cargo area and a step stool for the navigator to use while taking celestial readings through the turret on top of the wing. On long flights requiring a double crew the forward (A) compartment was reserved as a crew rest area with three bunks. This was the first Boeing airliner to have a circular staircase, the one climbing to the flight deck. They later used one on the B377 Stratocruiser leading down to the cocktail lounge, and still later on the 747, leading up again to the flight deck and the upper passenger cabin.

Probably the high point in the history of the Boeing Clipper came in January 1943, when, in great secrecy, one of them flew President Roosevelt across the South Atlantic from Miami to North Africa. While the airplane and crew waited at Bathhurst (south of Dakar) the President went on to Casablanca on an Air Force Douglas C-54 for a lengthy meeting with Winston Churchill and Charles De Gaulle. The same aircraft and crew then flew the Presidential party back to Miami, celebrating the president's birthday enroute. The *Dixie* Clipper was, effectively, the first Air Force One.

The B314 was a very luxurious airplane, with every passenger convenience. The cabin was heated and had a thermostatic temperature control, hot and cold water in the bathrooms, large curtained berths, and a full galley to provide hot meals. The exhausts were at the top of the engines, so that the insulated cabin areas were very quiet. Maximum seating capacity was 71 people, but I do not think that number was ever achieved in service, except possibly on the New York-Bermuda route, because of weight limitations. When the war ended in 1945 most of the military contracts were terminated, but the Boeing Clippers maintained a daily schedule to Honolulu until

1946, as many high priority military passengers still had to be carried back and forth. The new Constellation aircraft would be arriving soon, and many war surplus Douglas DC-4s were available, but for a few months the old Boeings soldiered on. I made my last trip on the Boeing on April 9, 1946. It was also the last commercial flight of a Pan American B-314. The foreman of the beaching crew was a colorful character named "Shorty" Greenough, and when I disembarked from that final flight he was standing on the dock with tears streaming down his cheeks. After we stepped off the *American Clipper* (NC18606) at San Francisco the airplane was taxied across the bay to Alameda Naval Air Station. Months later it was ferried to San Diego, to join the rest of the fleet on the surplus auction block. Pan American had the option of buying the airplanes back from the Navy for $1.00 each but had no use for them as the future was in land planes.

During the war adequate runways had been constructed at almost all of the island stations so there was no longer a need for a seaplane. The landplanes developed during the war offered greater reliability, speed, and range, so that after only a few years of service the flying boats were obsolete.

I had a dream a few months ago that sticks in my mind. In the dream I was at an air show displaying my beautiful "Tiger Moth" airplane, when Bill Gates (of Microsoft) stopped to admire it and talk with me. He asked me what I thought would be the "ultimate" antique airplane, and I replied that, without doubt, it would be the Boeing Clipper. Then he asked where he might buy one of them, and I explained that they were all gone, but I added, I think if you ask them nicely the Boeing Company will build a new one for you. They still have all the blueprints, and it would fit nicely into the backyard of your new home on the water. It was just a dream, but Bill Gates could well afford to do it.

CONSOLIDATED PB2Y3R
(Coronado)

Consolidated PB2Y3-R

Reuben Fleet, the founder of Consolidated Aircraft, built more flying boats then anyone else in the United States, but this was not one of his better efforts. He knew it, and did not want to continue with its development, but the Navy insisted because it needed a faster patrol aircraft than the aging Consolidated PBY. The PB2Y3 was a flying boat version of a B-24, with the same wing and engines (P&W R1830-88) but with a seaplane hull and retractable wing tip floats. It was an ungainly, crudely built airplane, but served its purpose, the transportation of manpower and supplies across the oceans. Pan American Airways flew them from San Francisco to the central Pacific via Honolulu, Canton Island, and Funafuti to Espiritu Santos. Another route was from Canton Island through Noumea, New Caledonia' to Brisbane, Australia. A daily service was maintained on both routes. Service was also established across the Atlantic from New

York to Foynes, Ireland. It was a very noisy, rough riding airplane. There is a saying that if you have enough horsepower you can make a barn door fly, and this is a good example of that idea.

The PB2Y3R had seats for 30 passengers, but the priority load was mail to the servicemen. GI's on Espiritu Santos loved us because they knew we brought their mail. One of the Coronados crashed on a night take-off from Funafuti lagoon when an unlit Liberty ship drifted into the seaplane area killing everyone on board except the Purser, Sam Toarmina, the Engineer, Terry Toles, and the Radio Operator, Larry Good. Sam was thrown clear, and survived with minor injuries. Terry went through the side of the airplane and was found floating in the water, still strapped to his seat. He survived, but his face still bore some scars. Rear Admiral Charles Cecil and his entire staff were killed.

MARTIN PBM3R
(Mariner)

Martin PBM3-R

The Martin PBM3R was the workhorse of the South Pacific. In spite of its size it was a rather graceful airplane in the air, and a very sturdy machine in the water. Because of its limited range these aircraft were based in Honolulu and only flown to the South Pacific islands. The Wright GR2600 engines were very powerful, but there were only two of them. Before the war ended, the Navy ordered the company to ferry the airplanes to Alameda. Because of the danger over such a distance, the company asked for volunteers to fly the ferry flights. The problem was that there was a two hour period in the middle of the flight during which if an engine failed the airplane would not have enough fuel to reach land in either direction. Yet when all the aircraft safely reached Alameda they were scrapped!

In the early design stages Martin built a 3/8 scale "proof-of-concept" airplane, powered by a 120 hp Chevrolet engine. The centrally-mounted engine drove the two propellers by means of long belt drives. With a slight bow to Pan Am, the Martin Engineering office nicknamed it the "Tadpole Clipper". It was good enough to permit Martin to start tooling for production before it had a military contract in hand. The Navy soon placed large orders, and many were built for the British forces. In the combat version the large nacelles behind the engines served as bomb bays, but in the "R" versions (transport) they were fitted with droppable fuel tanks. With 20 passenger seats we usually carried a mix of people, cargo, and mail.

The short exhaust stacks produced a powerful rumble, and a colorful display on the rare occasions that we flew at night. At take-off or climb power, with the mixture controls in the "Full Rich" position, there would be a long tail of red and yellow flame behind the engine. As we leveled at cruise altitude and the mixture controls were leaned to cruise settings the color of the flames changed to orange and then to a short "spitting" blue color, only a few inches in length. The sound of the exhaust smoothed, the vibration lessened, and there was a contented sound to the engine. The Flight Engineers station was located in the right rear of the flight deck, with a window looking at the right engine, so I had a close view of the effect my mixture controls had on the engine.

In recent years the scaled-down prototype was restored by volunteer Martin employees and given to the Smithsonian's National Air and Space Museum. It is now on display at the Baltimore Museum of Industry.

PACIFIC STATIONS

PEARL HARBOR

After five months of training I was sent to the Pearl Harbor base in Hawaii for a six-month assignment. To get to Hawaii I was scheduled as the Assistant Engineer on the *China Clipper*, but I had a small problem. I didn't have my "Blue" uniform yet, only the Khakis. So the office told me to wear a suit, so as not to confuse anyone. The flight took twenty-two and a half hours. With a four hour "watch schedule" I worked about 12 hours at the Engineer's station, but was in the cabin for landing. As we rounded Diamond Head, descending for landing at Pearl Harbor, the Purser, Barney Sawicki, moved me to the main cabin, and told me that I would be the first to disembark. He handed me a ten-dollar bill, and asked that I give it back to him as I left. When the engines had been shut down and as the aircraft was towed backwards to the dock, all 15 or so passengers were standing behind me. Barney carefully maneuvered me so that they could all plainly see me give back his "tenner", and they all dug in their pockets. Some of those Pursers made more money than the Captains.

We had company quarters in the old Dillingham family summer home on the edge of Pearl Harbor, with a company mess hall nearby. Our time was split between flying assignments and aircraft maintenance work. After a trip we had a day off, then picked up our toolboxes and did maintenance work until the next flight assignment. Most of the heavy PBM maintenance was done across the harbor on Ford Island, but routine maintenance was accomplished at the Pearl City terminal docks. Work on engines was done with the help of small platforms hung from the side of the engines, about fifteen feet above the water. In the balmy Hawaiian climate I usually only wore shorts, sandals, and a T-shirt. If a wrench, or an engine part was dropped you just followed it down into the water and grabbed it before it sank out of sight. Then climb back up to the engine stand and go back to work. On a really warm day I might make four or five such retrievals.

Wartime rationing allowed each of us a bottle of hard spirits or a case of beer per week. The company thoughtfully provided us with a large two-door refrigerator, which barely served the twenty or so of us. As our quarters and meals were provided, the salary was adequate. Our pay was the same as a Navy Ensign, which had just been raised to $154 a month.

Next to the large rambling Dillingham house was a dirt volleyball court, with a full view of the busy Pearl Harbor. A daily company bus took us to downtown Honolulu and Waikiki for a little recreation on the occasional day off, since there was nothing available in nearby Pearl City. Every morning two large Hawaiian ladies arrived about 8 AM to make the beds, sweep the floors, and complain about the messy slobs they served, although they were good humored about it. Bill Newport, one of the senior Engineers, was our godfather and supervisor—a task he took slightly seriously. At least once a week Bill joined us in the lounge area for a few hours of poker and jokes, and to review our training curriculum progress.

PALMYRA ISLAND

Palmyra is a delightful coral atoll, with a few thin groves of pine trees. Officially the island is a part of the Hawaiian Islands, but is privately owned. There was a small Navy base there, primarily to service seaplanes, and a short coral runway, suitable for a DC-3. Far from any part of the war, it must have been a desirable, but lonely assignment. We used it as a refueling stop for the PBM-3 aircraft.

CANTON ISLAND

Canton was the hub of South Pacific (SOPAC) and Central Pacific (CENPAC) operations. The pre-war Pan American hotel was still there and served as our dining room and lounge. A vast and beautiful lagoon served as our runway, and also provided all the fresh fish one can imagine. The lagoon was a giant, crystal clear, salt-water swimming pool. We devised some primitive swim goggles and snorkel tubes to enable us to explore the marine life around the coral heads.

The overnight facilities were little more than cots in Quonset huts, but were adequate. It was here that I learned to hate Spam and dried eggs, and to relish pickles. On one trip Admiral Halsey joined us in diving off the wing tip of our PBM, then climbing up through the waist hatch to do it again! Some nights "Bed Check Charlie" a Japanese observation plane, flew over at about 10 PM (probably from Tarawa) and when he left most of us retired for the night.

The island is jointly held by the United States and Great Britain as a "condominium", the result of conflicting claims made in the mid 1930s when Pan American and British Overseas Airways were doing surveys for Pacific flights. The British Navy and the U.S. Navy made near simultaneous landings, and the two nations diplomatically decided to share the Island. On the British side of the dividing line their representative had a small house and post office, and carried on alone in the midst of the war. Both governments installed flagpoles adjacent to the dividing line.

The "Cannonball" concept was that the airplane kept going, changing crews as needed, so we normally had a 24-hour layover every time we landed at Canton. There would usually be five or six crews there at any time, enough to work up a softball or volleyball game. In the evening an old movie was shown in the hotel lounge. The Seabees had built a runway on the high side of the island, and there was a constant flow of military aircraft heading for the combat zones, and ambulance planes returning the wounded. Since Canton was the only feasible refueling stop in the central Pacific there were a lot of aircraft passing through.

WALLIS ISLAND

Still ruled by a few French administrators, but greatly outnumbered by the U.S.Navy and The Seabees, Wallis was not an atoll, but a true island, and very attractive. One night I attended a graduation ceremony at the Catholic girls high school ("The Virgin Village"), where we were treated to their version of the "Siva Siva" dance, a sort of hula. Another night a native tribe invited us to a party, where I was introduced to "Kava". As we sat in a circle around a fire, one of the tribesmen ground some roots in a bowl, squeezed out the juice, and passed coconut cups to us. One by one we were expected to drink from the small cup. I cannot remember the taste, but I do remember that I could not feel my feet on the ground as I floated back to our quarters! Early evenings the sky filled with hordes of fruit bats with a wingspan of about 18 inches! One of the Seabees was a man named "Louie", who operated a still up in the hills. He had developed a way to make a form of "Okoolihau", the Hawaiian fermented drink. Instead of pineapple, Louie used dried fruit; apricots, raisins, apples, or almost anything else that came to hand. When Louie learned that he had come down with "Moo-Moo" (Elephantiasis) he was the happiest man on the island because the cure was to be sent home to Chicago.

SUVA

The "Jewel of the South Pacific", Suva is a lovely city on the southeastern shore of Viti Levu, the largest island of the Fiji group. The Grand Pacific Hotel was properly British and very impressive, with a sweeping view of the harbor a few blocks below. A roofed-over porch ran around two sides, so one could enjoy tea (or beer) even on a rainy day while watching the busy harbor. It was here that I first became aware of the Fijian people, a race I came to admire greatly. The local policemen, in white "Lava lavas" (skirts) and huge "beehive" hairdos, were the most dignified, powerful people I had ever seen. In later years I came to know them better, and to this day I can still recall their singing voices, their happy faces, and their tender ways. If you ever have the chance to hear a Fiji group singing their national song, "Isa Lei", pay attention.

AUCKLAND

We operated one trip a week to paradise on the PBM aircraft, and you had to wait your turn. It was an overnight stay at the Durant Hotel or the Star Hotel, which were only a few blocks away from the Peter Pan Ballroom, where a hundred lovely young girls were waiting. Most of the young New Zealand men were away in the service, so we were made to feel very welcome. My first trip to Auckland was memorable. When three of us were sent to the Durant Hotel, the two pilots simultaneously complained to the desk clerk of a cold, both saying they should have the odd "single" room. The clerk asked me if I felt all right, and I said I did. He said; "Fine, we will put you in the single room, and let these two "sickos" share their misery." After a grand night out, on the next early morning I discovered that the airplane's center hull fuel tank rubber lining had disintegrated and there were rubber particles floating about in the fuel. So back to the Durant we went for eight days, while we waited for a new tank liner to be sent from Baltimore. I was a hero to the other members of the crew. The main complaint about the hotel was that there seemed to be no way to stop the maids from bursting into your room at seven AM with a tray of tea and biscuits.

The people who settled New Zealand brought everything that was English with them, and they have clung to their ancestral traditions. The game of rugby, as played by the "All-Blacks" national team is almost a religion, as is soccer. Lawn bowling is as traditional as the tea ceremony. To the great credit of the authorities the native Maori people are respected and encouraged to keep their traditions and history alive. I once did a three-hour drive with a Maori chief, and he entertained me for half an hour reciting his family history, name-by-name, dating back to the arrival from Tahiti. He said that he had to keep practicing for fear he might forget part of it.

In later years one of the Pursers, in making the pre-landing announcement, put it this way;

"Ladies and gentlemen, we will be landing at Auckland International Airport in 25 minutes. As you know, there is a time difference between Fiji and Auckland. Please set your watches back fifty years."

BRISBANE

This was sometimes a difficult port. A seaplane is essentially a sailboat, and the combination of wind, tide, and current can make it a real handful to operate. After landing, the Third Officer had to stand in the bow door and snag the line attached to an anchored buoy, then hook it over the aircraft bow post. Once attached to the buoy, a small boat came along to attach a stern line to the shore or another buoy. Drifting down the Brisbane River at idle power, with a following wind, could mean you were moving pretty fast, and that buoy went by very quickly. If your throw with the grappling hook missed, the pilot had to gun the engines and maneuver to take another run at it. After the third or fourth try the atmosphere on the flight deck got a bit frosty. Brisbane was a rather dull industrial town in the middle of a war. Ushers Hotel was adequate, but it was hard to find anything on the dinner menu that didn't bleat.

FUNAFUTI

A part of the Ellice Island group (now called Tuvalu), Funafuti was a lovely tropical atoll, obliterated by war. We had to stay here for 24 hours, which was probably too long. The Japanese dropped "grass cutter" bombs that spread shrapnel laterally, so as to inflict maximum casualties on personnel, and scarcely a palm tree was still standing. We slept in a Quonset hut next to slit trenches because the Japanese bombed almost every night. Although the Marine Corps had a squadron of F4U fighters equipped with all the latest night fighter equipment, not a single airplane flew. The island was ringed with anti-aircraft installations, but not a gun was fired. The military said they didn't want the Japanese to know what weapons they had. Fresh water was available for drinking only, so we soon learned to bring a bar of salt-water soap, and carry our laundry on with us. One evening I was standing, shoulder deep, in the lagoon with three or four others, when a large shark passed between us. I was so startled that I was the last one out of the water.

My crew was called out one early morning to make an unscheduled trip to Tarawa, about six hundred miles north of Funafuti. The Second Marine Division had landed there four days earlier, and we were to pick up the Brass and fly them to Canton Island on their way to Pearl Harbor. We landed shortly after dawn, as the bulldozers were burying the dead, and took on about fifteen or so Marine officers, including Major General Julian C Smith, Commanding Officer. The crew always ate first, so a few hours after takeoff I was the last of the crew to go below for breakfast, and the General and two "Bird" Colonels joined me at the small table. I will never forget sitting there and watching as the General laced his fried eggs, potatoes and bacon with catsup and then gave them a good stir with his fork. Then the two Colonels did the same thing.

The battle for Tarawa was touted in the news as a great victory, and I guess it was—but at a terrible cost. More than two thousand Americans were killed and 4,000 injured. The Japanese forces and Korean laborers defending the island were obliterated. Of the 4,000 Japanese troops only a handful survived. Because this was the first American attempt at a beach landing a lot of things went wrong. Poor communications, and a lack of coordination doomed many of the Marine units. The air support was ineffectual, and the Naval bombardment was badly executed. I am sure that General Smith and his staff had a lot of things to talk about when they reached Honolulu

NOUMEA

Noumea, New Caledonia was probably the furthest outpost of France, and suffering. Open sewers lined the sides of the streets, there was little food, and they were happy to have an American presence, if only to provide protection and supplies. Our overnight quarters were miserable, and the food was terrible, but it was only for one night.

ESPIRITU SANTOS

My memories here are mainly of mud, terrible rainstorms, and wind. This was the jumping off place for most of the forward military operations, so our support was critical, if only for the mail. I had never seen mud two feet deep before. At the Officers Club a mixed drink was 15 cents, and a beer was a dime, as was a pack of cigarettes. The supply clerk there could provide you with almost any uniform article you wanted, at no charge, but when I asked for a "Halsey Cap" I had to slip him a fiver to get it. During a violent storm one of our aircraft could not get into the harbor area to land, so it landed in the open sea instead. It took the crew ten hours to taxi the plane into the harbor, and every man was violently seasick.

LINE OPERATIONS

Early in 1944 1 returned to San Francisco and in a few months acquired my Aircraft and Engine Mechanic licenses and became a fully qualified Flight Engineer. At that time there was no such thing as a Flight Engineer license, so in later years when the FAA created that license, they just sent me one in the mail. The FAA reasoned that because we had been working at the job for years, there was no need to examine us.

BOARD AND LODGINGS

On arriving back in San Francisco I put up in a hotel for a few days while looking for a place to live. One of the other returning Engineers, Joe Salerno, teamed up with me and together we found a room in a boarding house on Jones Street in the city. The owner, Mrs. Gainey, showed us through the place in the morning and we moved in that afternoon. She told us that the dinner chime would sound at 6:30 p.m., and that gentlemen were expected to wear coats and ties. When Joe and I strolled into the dining room, properly attired, it was a pleasant shock to discover that we were the only "gentlemen" in the place. The rest of the tenants were young ladies who had come to San Francisco to work in the big city. There were about 30 of them. Joe and I immediately

spread ourselves around to bring as much joy as we could to
their lonely lives. The boarding house also featured a large,
jovial, Swedish cook who spoiled us. Joe and I shared a large
room and bath, but seldom saw each other as the airline
worked us rather hard. The salary was still low, but I found
that with my Naval Reserve ID card I could bypass the unions
and work at the waterfront warehouses. A twelve-hour night
shift in a meatpacking warehouse paid me the equivalent of
a week's salary at the airline. After six months I had lost 15
pounds, and I think Joe had gained the same amount. When
my mother moved to New York, I took over her flat on Pacific
Avenue, but Joe stayed on at the boarding house for years,
until transferring to Seattle after the war. My mother set me
up with a clothing salesman from Roos Brothers department
store as a housemate to defray expenses. Most of his social
activities were in Sausalito, across the bay, so I seldom saw
him.

I was then 22 years of age, and soon my salary was raised
to $220 per month. Miss Valeda Lee, in the Chief Pilot's
office, did all the crew scheduling. (and almost everything
else in that office). The usual assignment was a shuttle to
Honolulu and back on the B-314, or to Honolulu on the B-
314 and then fly several trips to the South Pacific on the
PBM, returning to San Francisco on the B314. Or it might
be a trip to Brisbane or Espiritu Santos on the PB2Y3.
Between trips we were expected to qualify in the different
maintenance shops. I had to demonstrate to "Pop" Eubanks
that I had a satisfactory knowledge of propellers. It took two
weeks to convince "Mac" McDonald that I was knowledgeable
on Accessories and Carburetors. The same for Aircraft
Controls, power plants, and Instruments. And in our spare
time we had a series of written examinations to pass every
six months to earn the next $25 per month pay raise.

As we had not worked our "way up" through the shops
my group was at first looked down upon by the old-timers
because we were not licensed mechanics as yet. We were

referred to as "Rocket Rangers". Engineer Nels Wicklund looked in the door of one of our classes and saw about twenty young students there. He turned to another Engineer and said we looked like a bunch of rocket rangers, conjuring up memories of the Flash Gordon comic strip. Strap us onto a rocket and send us off to war. The name stuck, and to this day those of us who are left are proud of it. I think it was a friendly term, because every man I met along the way was supportive and eager to teach. Once established, the job was very pleasant, although the hours were long and hard. The FAA had loosened the time limits during the war, so we could fly up to 120 hours per month, and we did

MOANA HOTEL

The company supplied adequate layover accommodations and paid us a per diem amount on most layovers to cover meals and tips, and paid for our laundry and uniform dry cleaning. The fifth and sixth floors of the Moana Hotel were our home in Honolulu. The Pan American laundry room in the hotel was incredible. A crew member might drop his laundry in the box, transfer to Miami, and come back five years later to find clean shirts waiting for him. On several occasions I was caught short by a schedule change and needed some clean shirts. A quick browse through the laundry room would always turn up a package of laundry belonging to someone I knew to be my size. Thus it was a swap of dirty for clean, and no harm done. Waikiki Beach, although lined with barbed wire, was delightful, and almost deserted. Adjacent to the hotel was the old Outrigger and Canoe Club which graciously extended complimentary memberships to the crews, so we could enjoy volleyball, surfboards, and outrigger canoes. The large old Moana Hotel dining room had not yet washed away, and that is where we took our meals. Several large round tables were reserved for PAA crews, and for three meals a

day we had the same Filipino waiter, who never took a day
off. PAA paid for the meals, but we were expected to leave
a generous tip. I heard that after the war that waiter went
home to Manila a relatively wealthy man. I found myself away
from home about 23 days a month. That was all right with
me since I was single, but it must have been hard on the
married men. A month's vacation every year, but at the
bottom of the seniority list that usually meant the very early
part of the year. Being a skier, I could live with that.

AIRCRAFT MAINTENANCE

Flight Engineering was considered a part of the
Maintenance department, at least as far as the "Table of
Organization" was concerned. The Operations Department,
through the Chief Pilot's office, had a strong voice in all
operations of the airline but I answered to Chief Flight
Engineer Carl Green, and he answered to the head of
Engineering and Maintenance. I even had a seniority number
in the shops, which came in handy when the war ended and
the cutbacks came. A new apprentice mechanic would
inevitably ask his foreman what he had to do to become a
Flight Engineer, and would be told to "get on the waiting
list". He then went upstairs to the office of big, gruff, John
Boyle, the head of Maintenance. John would take out a paper
from a bottom drawer and enter a new name at the bottom
of the long waiting list. It was a great morale builder, and
gave the apprentice a real incentive to study. Carl Green,
and his assistant (and later Chief Flight Engineer) Al Loeffler,
ran a very benevolent department. If you had any sort of a
problem they were ready to help. There was a feeling of
mutual support from every member of the department, and
in a short time the term "Rocket Ranger" felt more
comfortable. Shortly after returning from my assignment in
Honolulu, I was scheduled for a 6:00 a.m. departure on the

PB2Y3, with Al Loeffler, the Assistant Chief, as the other Engineer. My alarm clock let me down, but I awoke at 5:00 a.m., called the company and made a frantic dash to Treasure Island. The airplane was straining at the pelican hook, with all engines running, when I threw my bags aboard and followed them into the waist compartment. I fully expected to be fired. Al just smiled at me and said; "Tom, I think you should have two alarm clocks".

In the brief years of operation before December 7, 1941 the maintenance procedures had been almost leisurely. With three B-314s and two M-130's available, and only a weekly flight to Manila and a weekly flight to Aukland, there was plenty of time for thorough maintenance. On arrival from Honolulu the aircraft was attached to its beaching gear, and towed up the ramp and into the hangar for scheduled maintenance. Huge work stands, specially constructed, were wheeled into place around the engines and a large crew of specialists went to work. The stands were equipped with all the special tools and parts needed, as it was a long trip up and down the metal ladders. There were even "lapping plates" at each engine position. The rocker box covers had to be removed to check intake and exhaust valve gap settings, and those covers had to be hand "lapped" level before being reinstalled. The nuts holding them secure would distort them enough to prevent an oil tight seal on assembly, so the mechanic hand polished them on a steel plate, laced with oil and fine emery. It was intended that the mechanic would not need to make many time-consuming trips up and down those long stairs. Before launching back into the bay the hull was sprayed with a coating of pure, hot, lanolin to protect it from salt water. While working in the shops I had the opportunity to perform this task. I left my arms bare but wore goggles and protective clothing. When I finished I was covered with about an eighth of an inch of lanolin wax (derived from wool), which I carefully peeled off and returned to the "hot pot", but I left the stuff on my arms through lunchtime. I have never had such beautiful skin! I was told that it cost about fifty dollars for all that lanolin.

When the maintenance department had completed the aircraft service the two Flight Engineers who were assigned to the next trip were notified, and the day before departure, came to the base to inspect the airplane. They donned white coveralls, and carried gas-proof flashlights and inspection mirrors. After reviewing the maintenance logbooks with the shop foremen, a thorough inspection was made, with emphasis on any discrepancy repairs. If the airplane was back in the water, a full power engine run would be performed. Any discrepancies they found were noted and a list given to maintenance for their correction. With the war on, the Clippers were restricted to San Francisco-Honolulu routes and the preflight inspections became more casual, just a one-hour pre-flight inspection done by the two Engineers. On the departure day the Engineers checked in at the Dispatch Office, where they were given a copy of the Flight Time Analysis, preliminary Weight and Balance, and the Fuel Loading form. After checking the paper work they proceeded to the airplane to do a full preflight check. The front wing spars of the airplane were of riveted aluminum tubing. and in most of the aircraft had developed some short, hairline cracks. Boeing felt that they were not dangerous, and did not want to compromise the integrity of the metal by welding the cracks, so we were required to measure each crack before and after each flight. That meant one of the engineers, while doing the preflight inspection in the wing tunnels, had to crawl beyond the outboard engines to measure the cracks and log them in a book. When the pre-flight inspection was completed, the senior engineer signed the maintenance logbook, accepting the aircraft as airworthy. Then the two engineers went back into the terminal, along with the radio operators, navigator, and stewards (who had been performing their own preflight activities). Now there was a Captains briefing, and sometimes an oral test on emergency equipment. When all was ready, everyone fell in, two abreast, behind the Captain and First Officer. The Captain gave a signal, one bell was sounded, and we marched to the airplane.

As the airline was operating under a military contract, the passengers and cargo were supplied by the Navy, and were carried as space was available. Many of the passengers were civilians on government business, lots of Navy brass, as well as an occasional ordinary sailor. Everyone received the full luxury treatment.

CASTING OFF

The Check Lists we had were casually used, if at all, but once settled in on the flight deck, and with confirmation that all were aboard and hatches closed, the Captain gave the order to prepare for departure. The beaching crew cast off all lines except the pelican hook. This was a "trip" hook clipped to the hull just aft of the step, and attached to a stout cable anchored on the shore. Inboard engines were started first to prevent too much side-drift of the aircraft. With all engines running well, a thumbs-up signal was given from the flight deck, the pelican hook was tripped, and we were under way. There was no intercom with the beaching crew, and the only radio communication was with the launch and PanAm Operations. Since a piece of driftwood could ruin ones day, the launch checked the buoy-marked seaplane lanes and gave us an "all clear" before we started take-off. When airborne one of the pilots called "Panop" on 2870 Kilocycles and gave them our take-off time. Enroute radio communications were handled by the Flight Radio operator, using Morse code on CW (Continuous Wave). A few of them still used the old-fashioned telegrapher's key, but most were using a modern high speed "bug".

CREW PROTOCOL

Cockpit discipline was variable. Captains who were easy going, nice guys on a PBM or a PB2Y3 in the South Pacific could be tyrants on a B314. 1 had trips on which I had to ask the First Officer's permission to speak to the Captain. There were two uniforms; the traditional Navy blue double-breasted one, but with collar bars instead of sleeve stripes. The Blue was worn only on the B-314 and M130. On the Navy aircraft the uniform was khakis, with collar bars and a navy leather flight jacket. Everyone's attitude seemed to change when they put on the "Blues". The Captain addressed me as "Mr. Engineer". He always knew the First Officer's last name, and addressed him as "Mr. Whatever". As well as you might know him, and in spite of how many beers you had shared the previous night, the captain was addressed as "Captain", or "Sir". On the Naval aircraft the atmosphere was more relaxed. First names, or nicknames, were in order, and if you didn't know the man's name you called him "Sparks", or "Magellan", or whatever nickname came to mind. I can remember "Skinhead", "Shorty", "Gassy", "Stud", two "Wicks", and lots of 'Buds". Morale was fantastic because everyone was so proud and pleased with what they were doing.

The long trips across the vast reaches of the South Pacific were very wearing as we would frequently be on duty for 12 or 14 hours at a stretch. We kept a running tab on the gin rummy and cribbage games, and the debts might mount up into the hundreds of dollars, but were always eliminated on the final leg of the trip with a few double or nothing bets. To relieve the boredom we sometimes traded jobs for a short time. I would take over navigation while the Copilot ran the Engineers station. The Captain manned the galley while the Steward sat in the copilots seat, and the Radio Operator flew the airplane as the Navigator handled the radio. All, with supervision of course. These trips would sometimes last for two or three weeks, back and forth from Honolulu to the South Pacific before we finally headed home to San Francisco, so we came to know each other very well. Of course, the home folks knew more about the progress of the war than we did. There was absolutely no news available out in the ocean, and the best we could do was an occasional copy of one of the Honolulu papers or the *Stars and Stripes*. After three weeks of flying I would have a week or so off before my next assignment. Time to have my laundry and cleaning done, visit my family, and prepare to go again. And during all this time I was, effectively, a civilian. My neighbors considered me to be a draft dodger, and people on the street asked why I was not in uniform.

The round, or Radial engine has a weak point, in that it is possible for oil to creep past the rings of the lower cylinders and partially fill the combustion chamber of a cylinder. This hydraulic lock could cause severe damage to the engine if it were struck with the force of cylinder combustion. (if the engine fired) This is easy to determine with a land plane by manually pulling the engine through a couple of revolutions. But it is difficult to do with a seaplane, because there is no place to stand. It was a rigid rule that the engine was turned through at least two revolutions with the starter before fuel was introduced for starting. The pilot on the appropriate side counted blades as the prop turned, and the engineer supplied fuel when assured that the cylinders were clear. A sudden stoppage was not disastrous if there was no combustion. This meant that the pilots took turns operating the start switches, while the other watched out his side window and announced the blade count. The Engineer looked out the side windows of the flight deck and handled the mixture controls and throttles. When the aircraft was nearing the takeoff area the pilot turned into the wind and called for a run-up check. The engines were checked two at a time, inboards, or outboards, together. Constant speed props were exercised from high to low pitch to cycle warm oil to the dome, temperatures and pressures checked, and the magnetos checked.

TAKE-OFF PROBLEMS

A calm day was pleasant, but provided a problem. Flying boats cannot take-off easily in smooth water because of the inherent drag of the sea water, making it difficult to get the airplane up onto the "step" and "planing". At San Francisco Bay on these occasions we would sometimes send the two Chris-crafts out to weave ahead of the Clipper in the hope of roughing up the water enough to allow a little air to squeeze under the hull and separate the aircraft from the sea. The take-offs were long. Three or four minutes at take-off power was normal, the engine time limit at full power being five minutes. Night takeoffs were difficult because the spray from the bow wave over the cockpit windows reduced visibility for the pilots to almost zero. Night take-offs were usually only made out of San Francisco because it was one of the few places where adequate radio aids were available. On a typical night departure from San Francisco Bay the Radio Operator was strapped into a standing position, under the Radio antenna loop. As the take-off progressed he called out bearings from the local radio stations to the Navigator. The Navigator plotted them on a special chart of the bay and called out heading changes to the Pilot. The Pilot made corrections to his heading by reference to the Directional Gyro, as the compass jumped about too much to be of use. We all hoped that some ship had not slipped anchor and drifted into the seaplane lanes. The most critical part of any flight is that long stretch of full power on take-off. If any failure is imminent, that is when it is most likely to occur. Once reduced to climb power everyone relaxed a bit and the rest of the trip was usually routine. Bucking the prevailing westerly winds, the crossing to Honolulu was sometimes made at altitudes as low as 500 feet. Those levels frequently had scattered clouds and slight turbulence, but the winds were friendlier. With a double crew, a watch schedule was established and posted. I think the hardest working crew members were the two stewards. On occasions we would have twenty or so passengers, and they had to do everything from scratch. No pre-cooked meals, no in-flight entertainment, just two guys, some raw food and a primitive kitchen. Many of them were veterans of the Matson boats to Honolulu, and did a fabulous job on the Clippers. Some of them were working second jobs in restaurants or bars in San Francisco. They were all colorful characters.

CRUISING

The usual routine on a long ocean crossing was Long Range Cruise. The most fuel efficient airspeed is 110% of stall speed, but this is very difficult to fly as the airplane is slightly unstable at such a slow speed. A slightly higher speed, around 115%, was usually selected. The basic idea of Long Range Cruise is that as the airplanes fuel is consumed and the gross weight decreases the airplane should fly at a slower speed to obtain maximum fuel efficiency. After leveling off at our cruise altitude we spent the next hours carefully reducing power, and airspeed, according to meticulous charts. When we neared our destination the engine RPM would be down to about 1400, and with a nose gear ratio of 16:7 the prop was only turning about 10 revolutions per second and could be seen. So we reached our maximum speed at the top of climb, and just kept slowing down for the rest of the flight.

In-flight routine was a full set of instrument readings every hour on a log book form, but the most important task was tracking fuel consumption. Fuel flow instruments gave

us the numbers to compute consumption, and this was
compared to fuel quantity guages as well as the bowser
readings. The bowsers were totalizing flow instruments. At
every navigation check point the Navigator advised the
Engineer of arrival time and the Engineer did a fuel
computation. When the time and consumption were
charted on the "Howgozit" chart it gave a graphic picture of
the flight's progress. During the first half of the flight the
focus was on the "Equitime Point", this being the point where
we were committed to continuing to destination or
returning. On some occasions the wind forecast was
incorrect, and having fallen far behind the flight plan
forecast, there was no choice but to turn around and go
back. After 18 hours in the air you would wind up back where
you started.

The mighty GR2600 Wright engines gave us little
trouble. At 1,500 horsepower they were the most powerful
aircraft engines built at that time, and as I recall we ran
them about 500 hours between overhauls. By modern
standards this seems rather low, but for pre-war and wartime
reciprocating engines this was typical. With the B314s four
big Wright engines there was an occasional fouled spark plug
or magneto failure. The wing access tunnel was a good
investment as it gave us access to the back of the engines in
flight to make repairs or adjustments. As the engines
approached overhaul time they sometimes built up lead and
carbon deposits on the exhaust valve stems, which could lead
to the valve sticking in the open position. This resulted in
backfiring and extreme roughness, but was easily remedied.
Throttle back, rich mixture, and as the cylinder head cooled
the valve resumed normal operation. Slowly open the
throttle to normal power, and lean the mixture to cruise
setting, and hope it did not happen again. As we got close
to landfall the whole cockpit crew started to search the
horizon. We all knew that Hawaii was there, but everyone
strained to be the first to see it. Before descent to landing,

the Engineer did a magneto check on each engine, and the off-duty Engineer scrambled out through the wing tunnels to manually close the shutters on the oil coolers.

I shall never forget the absolute silence on the flight deck as the airplane settled on the water. There was a slight shudder and a hissing sound as it planed on the step before settling and slowing. Then the only sound was the engineer ratcheting the cowl flaps open, and the grinding noise of the wing flaps retracting. We were all a bit numb after 18 or so hours in the air, and the long taxi to the dock at Pearl City was a real anti-climax. After a conference with the maintenance foreman we climbed onto the Navy bus and headed to the Moana Hotel for two days of rest, a bit of volleyball at the Outrigger club, and a fresh supply of laundry.

THE EXPERIENCE

Pan American had the reputation of having the best-trained flight crews in the world, and it was well deserved. In the early years of air transport operations, the Flight Engineers were little more than airborne mechanics, but the advent of large multi-engined aircraft demanded support for the pilots many tasks, and the Flight Engineer station was created on the M130 and the B314 for this purpose. Also, long-range operations across the Pacific and Atlantic Oceans required a more scientific approach to the economical operation of the airplane. The Operations Engineering department developed the techniques of Cruise Control, which were refined by the Flight Engineering department with the help of the engine and aircraft manufacturers. This was a somewhat radical change in aircraft operations, and PAA for a long time was the only company with the necessary expertise and experience. In 1943 the Navy was operating the same Consolidated PB2Y3R (Coronado) aircraft on routes parallel to PanAm across the

Pacific, but they consumed 30% more fuel from San Francisco to Honolulu, and accordingly, carried about 30% less payload. The Navy brass was not happy with this and asked Pan Am for help. I was one of those assigned to teach classes in Cruise Control and Howgozit to Navy flight engineers of the VR2 squadron at Alameda Naval Air Station. All of them were older Chief Petty Officers, most of them twice my age (22), and they were not too impressed by a young kid, like myself, trying to teach them something. When I handed out the Pratt and Whitney power plant charts, most of them broke for coffee. After three days of class they saw the light and became enthusiastic, especially at the prospect of reduced fuel consumption and more positive fuel reserves. The Navy pilots were another problem. The idea of "leaning" the engine mixture controls horrified them, and at first some would not allow it, but in a few short months the Navy squadrons equaled PAA's performance.

GENIUS

The initial Pan American service from Key West to Havana in 1927 had one glaring problem; navigation. The slow Fokker airplanes could readily drift far off course in tropical winds, even over that short 90 mile distance. Visibility was frequently poor in rain and clouds, and turbulence made it difficult to hold an accurate heading. Something had to be done or there would be disasters. Trippe called on RCA (Radio Corporation of America) for help, and they sent Hugo Leuteritz, who had been doing some experiments on radio direction finders. He developed a lightweight transmitter and receiver for the aircraft, and a direction finder by which a ground operator could track the airplane and send course corrections by voice radio. The pilots were not very receptive to the idea of somebody on the ground telling them which way to go, but the device soon proved its worth. After six months Trippe hired Leuteritz away from RCA, making him Vice-President of communications. Hugo went on to develop the Radio Direction Finder, making long-range over-water navigation feasible.

One of the first people Juan Trippe hired was a short, slender, balding Dutchman, Andre Priester, making him the Chief Engineer for the airline. Priester was an intense, demanding man who worried about everything. His thick accent made him difficult to understand at times, so people had to listen carefully to what he said, and although the language was awkward the message was clear; Do it my way, or get out. There was no compromise, and Trippe allowed him a free hand, or more accurately, two. Aircraft manufacturers, engine manufacturers, pilots, mechanics, nothing escaped his notice and his harsh appraisal.

The early freewheeling attitude of some of the pilots received his full attention, and soon they were wearing standardized uniforms, studying operating manuals, and attending classes. Priester himself enforced a rigorous code of conduct, and any serious infraction was cause for immediate dismissal. The pilots soon recognized that, because of his high standards, they were flying the best aircraft available, and Pan American maintenance was the best in the world. He soon became a legend, and almost loveable. Every crewmember was required to carry a Boy Scout knife on his person, even the cabin staff. If you reported for a trip and didn't have your knife, you would be replaced by a stand-by crewmember, so the secretary in the Chief Pilots office kept a few knives in her desk drawer. Naturally, we called the knife a "Priester", and everyone tried to imitate his accent. On the one occasion I met him, I was so awed and frightened by the man that I tried to stay out of sight.

Mr. Priester had signs made up and installed on many office walls that read;

*"Aviation is not in itself inherently dangerous. But to
an even greater extent than the sea, it is terribly unforgiving
of any carelessness, incapacity, or neglect".*
                                        Captain A.G.Lamplugh

In the 1930s air travel was regarded by most people as hazardous, if not dangerous, so Priester set out to create a favorable image to the public. Arrivals and departures became "show time", with the crews marching on and off the airplanes. The Captains were glamorized, the best example being Ed Musick, who soon became the most famous airline pilot in the world, even appearing on the cover of Time magazine and in the newsreels in theaters. It did not help Priester's campaign when Musick and his survey flight crew were lost in the Pacific. To further enhance the image, our instructions were specific; you were not to carry anything while in public view. Drop your luggage at the crew check-in area and it would be delivered to the airplane. On checkout from a layover hotel, leave your key with the bell desk, and your bags would be delivered to the crew bus. On disembarking the aircraft leave your briefcase on the dock and it would be taken to the crew bus. We were professionals, and should conduct ourselves accordingly in every way, even after a twenty-hour flight. The story is told that Mr. Priester was in San Francisco for a few days and observed the Clipper arrival at Treasure Island. The two Engineers stopped on the dock to talk to the maintenance representative, the Radio Operators stopped to chat with the radio mechanic, and the two Stewards talked to the people from Commissary. At the top of the ramp the Captain and First Officer detoured to greet their wives, and the remaining formation of three marched into the terminal. The Dutchman was irate, and the next day the Chief Pilot called the entire crew to report for some arrival training. The word soon got around.

Juan Trippe was the planner, the schemer, the secretive plotter who crreated the airline. Leuteritz and Priester were the practical geniuses who made it possible.

POST WAR

Crew of the last flight of a Pan American flying boat.
The author standing second from right.

With the end of the war in 1945 the Navy contracts came quickly to an end, and the Pacific Division suddenly shrank to a mere three Boeing 314 Clippers. In 1946 the first Lockheed Constellations were delivered, and the flying boats were retired. I was part of the crew on the last B314 flight from Honolulu to San Francisco, and then went into training on the "Connies". The three Clippers were taken across the bay to Alameda Naval Air Station, towed onto the ramp on beaching gear and sat there for a few months before being flown to San Diego, and the auction block. While in Constellation ground school I was called out one day to do an engine run on the Clippers. The engines had not been "preserved", so they had to be run at regular intervals to prevent corrosion and oil contamination. I reported in the morning, and with two mechanics drove a company truck to Alameda. While they stood fire watch I started the engines on each airplane in turn and gave them a 30-minute warm up.

Whenever a few of the old guys get together there is bound to be some talk about the "GOBD" (Good Old Boat Days)". Not that they were all that good, but they were certainly exciting, and they tend to stick in our rosy memories.

With the end of the war there was a major shift at Pan American. With runways built at most Pacific islands the future was in land planes—no more flying boats. Pan American had the opportunity to buy back the B314s for a dollar apiece, but declined. They were sold off by the government as war surplus for $50,000 each and soon disappeared.

The early Constellation aircraft were equipped with Wright R3350 engines, but they did not yet have direct fuel injection. Those carburetor—equipped engines would catch fire very readily, and did so often, especially on starting. The fire was serious, because the rear accessory case of the engine was a magnesium casting and burned with an unquenchable flame. A slight backfire on starting could burn the engine off the wing. One of the Engineers, "Doc" Savage, had a traditional red fireman's helmet he wore while starting the engines, but I don't think it helped. On one of my first trips to Honolulu on the Connie two engines failed en-route and we spent two weeks at the Moana Hotel waiting for spares.

We had lots of volleyball and beach time. The fire problem was so acute that the aircraft were grounded while Wright modified the engines, replacing the carburetors with direct fuel injection.

The transition from the slow-flying boats to that Lockheed hotrod was rather dramatic. The pilots suddenly found themselves coping with a machine that flew at twice the speed of their previous mounts, and reacted twice as fast. The Flight Engineers were coping with a pressurized airplane with a more complicated electrical system and very temperamental engines. One of my early training flights illustrates a typical problem. Captain "Jack" Tilton was one of the early Clipper Captains, and a model aviator. He had been the Chief Pilot at San Francisco for years and was everyone's idol. He was also one of the most civil, kind, and modest people I have ever known. Perhaps his only deficit was his enthusiasm for baseball. Between Honolulu and San Francisco he insisted that the operating copilot or radio operator monitor the radio broadcast of the SF "Seals" baseball game on KPO radio while Jack was off watch. The pilot or radioman had to take notes on the game so he could give a full report when Jack returned to the cockpit. With the advent of the Constellation, Jack was one of the first in line for training. Assistant Chief Pilot Bill Price assigned himself the task of indoctrinating Tilton, and I was assigned as the Engineer. Captain Tilton made a night take-off from San Francisco, and Price gave him headings to fly, telling him to go to the Sacramento area, where we would do some air work and some touch-and-go landings. We leveled off at about 9,000' and admired the evening sky and the lights below. After about 45 minutes Price asked how soon we would be in the Sacramento area, and Tilton's response was a vague; "soon", and he started peering out the window. Price laughed and said, "Jack, we just passed Reno".

A few weeks later I was scheduled for another training flight with Captain Nate Searles, who was giving an indoctrination flight to Captain Dent Terrel. Flight Engineer Bill Lincoln was also on board. This time the air work and touch and go's were done at Stockton Airport. As Captain Terrel flew back to San Francisco, Nate Searles said he would do the approach and landing to "keep his hand in". The approach and landing were normal, and as we rolled down the runway, Captain Searles made the standard "callouts"; "Props low pitch, cowl flaps open, flaps up!" I was already taking care of the props and cowls when there was a sudden sinking sensation! Captain Terrel, for the first time acting as co-pilot, had grabbed the wrong handle, retracting the gear instead of the wing flaps. Captain Terrel pushed the throttles full open, hoping to pull the airplane into the air, but Searles wisely closed them to avoid the damage and fire hazard of hitting the pavement at full power. As the airplane screeched and ground to a halt on its belly, Bill Lincoln opened the crew exit door on the right side and grabbed two portable C02 extinguishers. I turned off the "Master Switch" and closed the fuel valves, and followed Lincoln out the crew door. He went to the right, I went to the left, and finding no fire we met back at the exit door, which was now at a convenient low level. Looking in at the cockpit, the two pilots were still in their seats, talking about what had happened. Within five minutes an FAA man was there, and immediately escorted the four of us to a room in the terminal building where he had each of us independently write a report of what happened. The airplane came to a stop in the middle of the intersection of the two runways at San Francisco and shut the airport down for six hours until airbags were brought from Travis Air Force base to lift the airplane and put down the gear so it could be moved. In preparing his defense, Captain Terrel became so knowledgeable on the landing gear and hydraulic systems that he was named Assistant Chief Pilot, Technical. It cost more than $100,000 to repair the airplane.

The end of hostilities meant that building materials were again available and the influx of people into California began.

Millions of soldiers and sailors had passed through the Golden State during the war, and a lot of them decided that this would be a nice place to live. Many thousands of them left the cold northern climes, and the hot muggy areas of the south and came west. This soon created a housing shortage and the lumber business was booming. My father expected that I would quit the airline and come home to the family business, but before I was faced with a decision I had a reprieve, of sorts.

MILITARY SERVICE

After I received my discharge from the Navy Reserve, the Alameda Draft Board decided that, because I had not served 90 days of active duty, I was "One-A' material and drafted me into the Army. As I was employed in a "vital industry" I was supposed to be exempt, but Pan American's Personnel department had neglected to file the proper forms. I had flown 2,000 hours in the war effort, but they drafted me anyway. My father had a good friend who was an Army General, and dad complained to him about my being drafted. The General looked into it and said that, while I should not have been called, there was nothing that could be done about it now. They put me on a slow troop train to San Antonio, Texas. Six summer weeks of army Basic Training in Texas did not do much to improve my opinion of army life. At the end of the training, I received orders to go to Mississippi to join a Cavalry unit. I decided that I would rather serve around airplanes than tanks, so I went to the "Air Inspectors" office, showed him my Pan Am letters and licenses, and two days later I was transferred to the Army Air Corps and sent to Hamilton Field, north of San Francisco, for shipment overseas. For two weeks I shared a compartment with 247 other men on a cruise to Yokohama, where I was assigned to Headquarters Squadron at Tachikawa Air Base, west of Tokyo.

With the end of the war most of the qualified airmen had gone home, leaving a few "career" men, and a bunch of

young, untrained, draftees. Two days later I was made the
Crew Chief on General William's Curtis Commando C-46
aircraft, with a crew of five "mechanics", all of them 18 years
of age and fresh off the farm. It took us three months to
restore the airplane into first class flying condition, and
almost that long for the crew of Japanese workers to strip off
the olive drab paint and polish the exterior. Now it was the
pride of Tachikawa, and I was promoted to Corporal. The
Engineering Officer wanted to make me a Sergeant, but
could not get approval since I was a draftee. Once a month
we flew the General to Seoul for a staff meeting, and once a
month we flew it to Manila to buy a load of liquor for the
Officers Club. There were also a few training flights every
month. The General was about five feet tall and five feet
wide, so I kept a parachute stowed by the rear door with his
name on it, and adjusted to his size. In Manila I always bought
a few cases of Bourbon for the maintenance staff, and two
cases of cigarettes. One case was for myself, and one for the
co-pilot, who was the CID (Criminal Investigation
Department) Officer for the base. A day or two after getting
back he would lend me his personal, winterized, Jeep, and
tell me which guard gate would be unmanned that evening
so that I could take our cigarettes out and sell them to the
Japanese. With our illegal gains we always put ourselves up
at what remained of the Great Manila Hotel, rather than
the military quarters at Nichols Field. I passed on the whisky,
at cost, to the other men in my squadron to keep everyone
happy.

As winter neared I read in the *Stars and Stripes* newspaper
that the military All Japan ski championships would be held
in January at the "R & R" hotel at Shiga Heights Ski Resort.
I sent home for my ski boots, gloves, and goggles, and
entered. The Army skis I scrounged were designed for a
man with a 60 lb backpack, and were much too stiff for
recreational skiing, so I altered them in the woodshop and
fitted my boots to the bindings.

There were about 20 entrants, as I remember, three of whom had never been on skis in their life. No matter, to a G.I. it was five days of TDY (Temporary Duty) at a resort hotel, paid for by Uncle Sam. All they had to do was fall down a few times and get to the dining room on time. One of the other competitors was a Paratroop Captain from a regiment in Hokkaido, the northernmost island of Japan. He was a third-generation Japanese-American (Sansei) who grew up in the Seattle area and was an excellent skier, with Inter-Collegiate credentials. When he showed up in the dining room for dinner there was quite a stir. He was tall, almost 6 feet, and very handsome, with a neatly trimmed moustache. His uniform was impressive, with a chest full of combat ribbons, and medals. As a Staff Officer he had the loops of braid on one shoulder, and those high paratrooper boots were polished like patent leather and laced with perfect white laces. The dozens of young girls working in the dining room obviously thought he was the greatest thing they had ever seen, and if he smiled at one of them she dissolved and had to run from the room. During the races the Japanese spectators were cheering him on, and when he fell some rushed to help him up. I couldn't help puzzling about the reception he got from the native Japanese. If the war had gone the other way, and an American was serving in the Japanese Army of Occupation in America, would he have been given a similar reception? I think not. We talked about it at lunch, and he said it was a cultural difference, and that the Japanese people were more practical than the typical American. He added that being able to speak the language made a big difference, and that Sansei friends of his who didn't speak Japanese were given quite a different reception.

At the end of the three-day competition I was declared champion, and the Army made me a special consultant to the Eighth Army Winter Rest and Recreation facilities. So when the General did not need the airplane, and the Officers Club did not need the airplane, I roamed around among the three winter resorts the army had appropriated and "consulted". I was entitled to a private compartment on the trains, and a reserved room at the resorts. After a year of very enjoyable active duty I was offered a discharge, and happily took it. The General liked me and wanted me to stay in the service, offering a Master Sergeant slot and a 60-day re-enlistment furlough. Although this would have been attractive to many others in such a situation, I just laughed.

During my year in the Army I decided that I did not really want to work for my father. I enjoyed my job at the airline, and I was looking forward to flying over a peaceful Pacific Ocean. As the only child I really hated to disappoint my family, but I did not want to disappoint myself either. I think my father understood, as he had been through a similar battle with his father, and lost. I learned later from my stepmother that during the war my dad had gone to the library for books and done a lot of reading on aviation to try to understand what I was doing. He had maps marked with the routes I was flying, and the places I stayed. And he bragged about me to his friends.

With a Ruptured Duck veterans pin on my lapel I reported back to Pan American. The Clippers were gone, the Constellations had moved to New York, and the airline was down to a handful of war-surplus C-54 (DC-4) aircraft. About half of the maintenance department had been laid off and I did not have enough seniority to stay on flight status, so I spent four months in the paint shop. We had the task of developing masking patterns to apply the Pan American blue paint to the ex-military DC-4's. I set up a surveyor's level on a work stand, and with another man standing by the aircraft nose and talking on an interphone, marked patterns to enable us to paint horizontal stripes on a rounded nose surface. Copies were sent to Miami and New York, as the airline converted dozens of C-54 aircraft to civilian DC-4s. I was soon back on flight status on the DC-4 and flying to an entirely different Pacific area.

DOUGLAS DC-4

Douglas DC-4

By war's end the Douglas C-54 aircraft had been flying for four years in military service, some of them operated by PAA across the Atlantic and Africa, and was a well-proven machine. The 1450 Horsepower Pratt & Whitney Twin Wasp engines were now able to run over a thousand hours between overhauls, making them a reliable power plant as well as very economical for the airlines. Pan American bought surplus C-54's as fast as they were available, eventually purchasing over 90 of them, and with the demise of the flying boats the Douglas DC-4 became the backbone of the fleet. Bought as military surplus at bargain prices, the aircraft were given a complete overhaul and upgrade before being put into service. A complete new cabin interior and galley was fitted, the exterior polished and the blue Pan American insignia applied.

Shortly after the end of hostilities the airline started full passenger service to Tokyo, Hong Kong, and Bangkok, and south to Sydney and Auckland. A few ex-military pilots were hired, and then a whole lot more entered training as the schedules increased. Instead of 16 or 18 hours to Honolulu we were now able to reach Hawaii in only 12 hours from San Francisco and the aircraft reliability was much better.

The San Francisco base expanded rapidly. Everyone who had been laid off in 1945 was recalled, and by 1946 all departments were hiring. But there were a few down corners. The navigators who were hired and trained during the war were released. They were replaced by the ex-military pilots recently hired and trained, thus re-establishing the original junior pilot program. That former Air Corps Major was going to learn to be a navigator, and in time learn to be a co-pilot, and in a long time sew four stripes on his sleeve.

By 1949 the Radio Operators disappeared as well. Radio communications had improved enough during the war, and after, that it was possible to maintain voice radio contact all around the world. New radio equipment was installed, and old "Sparks" was gone.

The Pacific routes soon became a comfortable routine. We had decent hotels, familiar layovers, reliable aircraft, and interesting passengers. The American tourist had not yet discovered the world beyond Honolulu, so most of the passengers crossing the western Pacific were military or government, plus a few business people. We were always briefed before departure about our passengers, and we were careful not to step on any diplomatic toes. Madam Chiang Kai Shek flew with us so often that she usually specified which flight attendants she preferred, as did President Sukharno of Indonesia, and General Claire Chennault and his wife.

PEACEFUL PACIFIC

Honolulu was the hub, and the routes extended south to Canton Island, Fiji, and either Auckland or Sydney. The central Pacific route was from Honolulu to Midway, Wake, Guam, Manila, and on to Hong Kong. From Wake, the northern route was to Tokyo, then Shanghai and Hong Kong. Twice a week the round-the-world flight went to Bangkok, Rangoon and Calcutta, then on to New York. This was pretty exotic stuff after those years of wartime Quonset huts, and military mess halls. During those early years after the end of the war not everything was first class, but most of it was comfortable. The crews still stayed on the fifth and sixth floors of the venerable Moana Hotel, and had access to the Outrigger Club next door. "Duke" and "Sarge" Kahanamoku, the legends of Waikiki, were back on the club beach, and the Banyan Court at the Moana Hotel was again the center of the Hawaiian tourist trade. The Imperial Hotel in Tokyo was a bit faded, but still a fascinating place to stay. Frank Lloyd Wright did not design the hotel for tall Californians and the low doorways took their toll. The Peninsula Hotel in Hong Kong was first class, and an interesting place to stay with all manner of people passing through the lobby. One afternoon I found myself sitting at the lobby bar next to a high school friend from Modesto, who was there to deal in war surplus material.

Post war Asia was on the move. For a few years Pan American had the skies to themselves, but soon every country with Pacific interests wanted its own national airline to help squeeze some of those tourist and business dollars. President Juan Trippe took the high road, offering training and consultants to many new national airline endeavors. It was a profitable business and established good relationships with local governments. Pan Am was relatively unknown in Peoria or Memphis but was well known everywhere outside of the United States.

I found the places I flew to fascinating, but the trips were as long as three weeks away from home. The sleep factor is hard to recognize when you are young, but sometimes it caught up with me. Pushing along, for days at a time, I would sleep for 12 hours when given the opportunity, and wake up feeling guilty.

Hawaii slowly changed from a military to a tourist economy. It took a year for most of the military to go home, and the tourist trade was very slow to start. The barbed wire disappeared from Waikiki beach, and soon the *Hawaii Calls* radio broadcasts from the Banyan Court of the Moana Hotel began to bring a few tourists to Hawaii. Pan Am developed what they called Sleeperette Seats to lure a few more. The usual arrangement on the Douglas DC-4 aircraft was 30 luxurious, reclining seats, with each pair enclosed by curtains at night for sleep. As the flying time to Honolulu was around 12 hours by DC-4, this was a big selling point, and the passengers liked it. Soon the daily schedule became twice a day, and direct non-stop service from Honolulu to Los Angeles was added, then Portland and Seattle. The Moana, Royal Hawaiian, and Halekulani Hotels were the only quality hotels for a tourist to stay in, and they soon filled. That sparked a building boom on Waikiki that continues to this day. It was too good to be true for Pan American, and soon the Civil Aeronautics Board decided that United Air Lines should provide competition, and then later added Northwest Airlines. Without domestic routes to feed passengers from inland America, as did its new competitors, PAA began to lose market share and had to rely on passengers destined for the Orient and Asia for the bulk of its business. Every attempt to obtain domestic routes for the company was effectively defeated by the politicians and the domestic carriers, and every government agency seemed to enjoy the chance to oppose the company's applications for domestic routes. The people of Hawaii loved Pan Am because of its pioneering relationship, but on a practical basis United and Northwest offered a service with convenient connections beyond San Francisco or Los Angeles to inland cities. The Filipinos, Aussies, and the New Zealanders had fond memories of the historic moments that Juan Trippe's airline had provided them, but when their own international airlines came into being they were, of course, supported. And the same was true all over the world. Trippe had the reputation of riding roughshod through the corridors of Washington, and the airline had enjoyed a highly subsidized monopoly position, but he met his match in Harry Truman.

WAKE ISLAND

Wake Island, the isolated spot in the northern Pacific that Pan American had, in 1935, converted into a vital re-fuelling station for the first transoceanic service in the world is still to me the ultimate vacation resort. It is an atoll made up of three islands ringing a large, shallow, crystal-clear lagoon. Wake usually has sparkling blue skies, maybe a few scattered low clouds drifting by on a sea breeze, and a visibility of 50 miles. The war's end came abruptly, and in a short time the military disappeared for discharge and home, leaving many of their toys behind. Now the island was occupied by Pan American, a few government meteorologists, and a couple of FAA representatives. The military went home, but they left the lights on and it soon became our private playground. Dredging through the military equipment left on the island we managed to get a bulldozer working and tore into the Japanese underground headquarters, but found nothing there. We patched up an old Air Force observation plane and flew it, but with the nearest land, Midway Island, being about 1,500 miles away there was nowhere to go but around the island. A few military jeeps were pressed into our service to tow "aquaplane" boards along the edge of the lagoon. Skimming along behind the jeep at 20 mph you knew that it was not a good idea to fall down, because the water was less than two feet deep, and under that were coral heads. We spent two hours one afternoon picking pieces of coral out of Paul Kohler's backside with tweezers, and I still have bits of coral growing in the soles of my feet. The island was a scavenger's paradise, full of copper utensils made by the Japanese forces, army equipment, and an occasional unsettling discovery of human remains.

Bone fishing in the lagoon was very good, especially with land crabs as bait, or with fly tackle. The concrete bridge between Wake and Peale Islands had been bombed and broken, but it provided a sheltered area for swimming and water skiing, and the more ambitious fishermen had good results casting into the ocean with weighted lines. During the last years of the war, Wake was cut off and bypassed by the American forces as the American policy was to neutralize it. An occasional bombing run kept the runway closed, and no shipping could get through, so the occupying Japanese army of nearly 4,000 men had no support or supplies from Japan, and some actually starved to death. There is no fresh water supply, and their water distillation plants ran out of fuel, making a rainstorm a salvation. At war's end a peaceful surrender was readily negotiated. The Japanese Commanding Officer was tried for war crimes and hanged in Guam. He had ordered the slaughter of almost a hundred American civilian workers just days before the surrender.

In later years, a neighbor of mine, Addison Mooney, asked me about staying at Wake Island. He was in the insurance business in San Francisco, and because that business was not regulated in Guam and the Philippines, had developed a large clientele of conservative business people in that area. He made a lengthy trip there every six months to sell policies. Add loved any kind of water sport, was an avid fisherman, and on the one-hour fueling and crew change stops on Wake, was fascinated by the area. On approaching Pan American about staying over a few days, he was told that there were no facilities for tourists, and they would not write a ticket for a stopover. When he asked me about it, I jokingly said; "Just go for a long walk during the fueling stopover, hide under a Scaveola bush, and when you see the Stratocruiser depart, come back and complain". He did it, and told me it was the greatest vacation he ever had. He bought some shorts, "T" shirts and "go-aheads" at the little PX and hung up his business suit. It was three days before they could get him on an airplane to Guam, but the staff put him up in the crew quarters, fed him in the company dining room, and entertained him. They took him deep-sea fishing, bone fishing, and water skiing in the lagoon. He even played a nine-hole round of golf at the Low Tide Country Club. And the price was right. I warned him not to try it again, and asked him not to tell anyone where he got the idea.

Anyone with a sense of history has heard the story of the gallant defense of Wake by the U.S. Marine Corps and the civilian workers in December of 1941, and of their tragic defeat after two weeks of brutal fighting. It was one of the few positive, but tragic, events during those early days of the war in the Pacific, and became a national rallying cry. Thousands of men, Japanese and American, died on that small pile of coral. Now, a few short years later, it was just a fueling stop for the airlines.

While on a flight from Tokyo to Wake on a Douglas DC-7C airplane, the Captain, Clancy Mead, and the Co-pilot, Bob Dankers, had a lengthy discussion in the cockpit about the difficulties of flying a straight-in approach and landing to an island runway. With little visual reference of land or buildings, and without radio aids, it is difficult to judge the aircraft height relative to the runway. Clancy Mead had a wonderful, dry sense of humor and he said "Now that we beat that subject to death, why don't you show us how to do it, Bob?" In absolute silence Bob Dankers flew a perfect approach and landing. There was just a small squeak as the wheels touched the runway, and no need for reversing the engines or heavy braking as we coasted to the end of the runway and made the left turn at the end to the terminal. As we taxied in, Bob finally broke the silence, saying; "Clancy, I want to thank you. I think that is the first landing I have ever made without the Captain yakking at me all the way." Clancy said; "Well, I figured you could mess it up all by yourself, without any help from me." Bob Dankers bought the beer.

MIDWAY

Midway survived the war fairly well considering the level of fighting that went on. The Pan American Hotel was still there, and, in season, the albatrosses, or "Gooney Birds" still ruled the roost. With the faster land planes we rarely used Midway as a fuel stop, but pushed on to Wake for a crew change, so we seldom had a chance to lay over there. The Navy operated a little short-range radio station to provide a news broadcast and some musical entertainment for the personnel, and we would occasionally tune it in if we passed near the island. It became a routine to call the tower for a chat as we went by. The Navy tower operators were sitting there with nothing to do in the middle of the night, and it brightened their evening to have a chance to chat with one of the stewardesses. Many of the girls carried messages back to San Francisco to be relayed by mail or phone to their families. The other routine was to request that the radio station play *The Yellow Rose of Texas* for us. I'm sure some of the passengers must have heard our enthusiastic singing in the cockpit as Midway Radio faded out of range. During the two 24-hour layovers I had at Midway I was amazed at the bird life. The Gooneys were the top entertainment on the island, but there were also tens of thousands of fairy terns and sooty terns nesting all over the place, even in the middle of the runway.

GUAM

Guam took a heavy pounding, with a great deal of damage during the brief Japanese attack and landing, and a few years later, the American re-occupation. As the airline resumed service through Guam there were no hotels available, so a "Staff House" was set up to accommodate the westbound and eastbound layover crews. There were some decent beaches, and a few sightseeing sites, like the historic area of Agana, the capital city, and the Magellan landing site. The Staff House had a sand volleyball court and a barbeque area, but the heat and humidity usually kept the layovers quiet. On top of the hill above Agana was the Navy Command Center and the Admiral's quarters, and we had access to their Commissary and dining room, as well as the golf course. I found Guam to be a good place to catch-up on sleep, and review my aircraft manuals. Every four or five years a tremendous hurricane hits Guam and trims the trees and the roofs of the buildings, but I managed to avoid those exciting episodes. The economic salvation of Guam came in the mid 1970s when Pan American introduced a daily service from Tokyo on the new 747SP aircraft. Some genius in the

Marketing Department started touting Guam to the Japanese tourists as a tropical destination, less than three hours from Tokyo. The Japanese travel agencies got into the act and very soon new hotels were growing like mushrooms to meet the demands. Then it became the "in" place for Japanese honeymooners, and we frequently left Tokyo with 180 newly wed couples destined for a "romantic" Guam honeymoon. It completely changed the economy of Guam.

MANILA

The bitter fighting in the area of Manila was still very obvious when service there was resumed. The beautiful Great Manila Hotel was almost a hollow shell, so again a Staff House was established, while the hotel was quickly rebuilt. Almost immediately the enterprising Filipinos were back in business, producing lovely linens, embroidery, and woodcarvings. Thousands of war surplus Jeeps were quickly converted into colorful "Jeepney" buses, and reconstruction of the city started immediately. Our Staff House was a few blocks from the old part of Manila, and near many historical sites around the old Intramura walled city and the lovely Luna Park. Nearby were the Wak-Wak Country Club and the American Embassy. We always followed a frustrating round of golf with a wonderful pitcher of "Calamansi Juice" to restore our perspective. The Calamansi is a small variety of lime, and it must have taken hundreds of them, hand squeezed, to produce that pitcher.

After a 24-hour layover we were awakened at 5 AM for a dawn departure for Hong Kong, but the weather there was frequently miserable with ceilings below our 1,000-foot minimums. At the usual wake-up time there would be a pounding on my door, the lights would flash on, and the Filipino room boy would say; "Go back sleep, you no fly today", and turn out the lights and slam the door. Sure.

In later years we flew a number of military charter flights to Clark Air Force base, north of Manila. The only decent layover facilities were a two-hour taxi drive up into the mountains at Baguio, the "Summer Capital", where we usually stayed at the Baguio Country Club, a beautiful and very comfortable spot. There is a large selection of tourist sites available nearby, everything from woodcarving shops to a gold mine. At 5,000-foot elevation, Baguio is a paradise in a pine forest. Three days in Baguio was like a vacation, with wonderful food, tourism, and a pleasant climate, but I just could not solve those sand greens on the golf course.

During a lengthy layover in Manila my 747 crew members were eager to see whatever was available, so we consulted with Tony, who had a travel office in the hotel lobby. He set us up for a day trip to Pagsanjan Falls, south of Manila. The two pilots and myself were in the lobby at 7 AM, with twelve stewardesses in tow when the fleet of taxis drove up. Tony introduced me to a middle-aged American tourist named "Roger", and asked if it we would allow him to join us. Roger had recently been widowed, and had retired from his job and taken passage on a slow freighter around the world, while he considered his future. He came ashore in Manila for a few days, and hooked up with Tony. I directed Roger to one of the taxis, added two tall blond Swedish girls, and told him to take good care of them. The trip by canoe up the rapids to the falls is exciting, and after a rubber chicken lunch, the trip down the rapids is terrifying, but it made for a very good day. Roger smiled all the way, and joined us for dinner.

Tony had tried to get us on the daily trip to Corregidor but the boat was fully booked, however he came up with a good idea. We chartered the extra boat for the day and had our own private trip, at our convenience, for only a couple of dollars more. Roger was delighted to join us. On the island a tour bus and guide gave us an excellent education on what was another rallying cry for America in the early years of the war. Walking through the tunnels and barricades of Corregidor I could almost feel the presence of McArthur, Wainwright, and 10,000 American soldiers. The huge parade ground, lined with deteriorating four story barracks, was a ghost town, and for a moment I thought I heard the faint strains of *taps* in the distance. I gained a totally new perspective when we caught up with the other group touring the island. It was a tour group of Japanese, and we caught up with them at a site honoring the Japanese soldiers who died during the battles at Corregidor.

FIJI

During World War Two the Nandi airport was built near the villages of Nadi and Lautoka on the west side of Viti Levu Island, a full 100 miles from the capital city of Suva. With the end of the conflict it became Fiji's International Airport. When Pan American transitioned from the flying boats to landplanes they found there were no suitable hotels in that area so a company compound was established. Within walking distance from the airport a part of the old military base was purchased and remodeled to serve as quarters for the ground staff as well as the layover crews. There were some native type Buris (thatched huts) scattered on a lush hillside for the stewardesses, and a former barracks became the male crew quarters. The men's bath facility was about forty feet away, down a path, so it was a good idea to carry a flashlite at night since there were frogs everywhere.

The accommodations were primitive but comfortable, and we loved it! All of the staff employees were local Fijians and they treated us like family, calling us by our first names (Thomass) and laughing and joking with us. The crew lounge was a large Buri presided over by a huge local chief, who was a great source of war stories and native lore. I treasure the memory of sitting on a bench under the kitchen window and listening to the staff singing as the did the evening clean up. Such voices!

We were often there for several days so a few crew activities soon developed: An all day trip into the mountains to a waterfall for a picnic lunch. A trip on the tiny steam locomotive through the cane fields to the sugar mill and back. Or a morning round of golf at the nine hole Lautoka course. If you were the first to play it was necessary to pull a few frogs out of the hole before putting, as they settled there during the night.

Today one of the most successful pro golfers is Fiji native Vijay Singh. Since his father was a Pan Am mechanic he learned his game at the Lautoka course.

As the new and faster airplanes were put into service Fiji became just a fuel stop, and the crew pressed on to Auckland, Sydney, or Canton Island.

HONG KONG

Hong Kong was the most exotic and foreign place I had ever seen. The Peninsula Hotel in Kowloon is still a grand hotel today, as it was in 1947. The harbor was alive with every kind of ship you could imagine, including those of the Royal Navy, and for a few dollars we could hire a junk to sail us through the crowded harbor to the east side of Hong Kong island and the Repulse Bay Hotel for lunch. We would leave a bottle of whisky with the crew while we dined, and on our return they were usually drunk enough that we could sail the junk back to Kowloon without their help.

Visits to foreign cities and countries are much more meaningful if you have studied up a bit on their history, and Hong Kong is a good example. The tales of piracy, opium wars, and intrigue have been glamorized in books such as *Tai Pan,* and there is more than a grain of truth in them. The early exploits of Jardine and Matheson in those dark endeavors helped establish their powerful trading company and secure a British foothold in Hong Kong and Kowloon. James Clavell's book only thinly disguised their exploits. England still ruled the colony with a firm hand, and an Anglo could walk anywhere without fear, even along the docks. To reinforce that grip the Jardine Matheson Company fired a cannon at noon every day across Causeway Bay.

Within a few months the merchants were back in business as if the war had never happened. A walk through the streets of Kowloon was fascinating. Anything and everything was there to be bargained for. The tailor shops offered all the latest Scottish Tweeds, English Gabardines, Cashmeres, Chinese silks, Irish Linens, and overnight tailoring, including two fittings was available for a very low price. The antique stores were filled with wonderful goods that had been dug out of wartime shelter. I had eaten Chop Suey in San Francisco, but a seven-course meal in a first class Hong Kong restaurant brought a new appreciation of Chinese food, one that I still enjoy. Now under Chinese control, Hong Kong is still one of the most interesting cities in the world, as it is the center of the mixing of all the cultures of the Orient in a vast commercial enterprise.

The new airport on Lantau Island is not as convenient as the old one at Kowloon, but must be much safer. The old Kai Tak airport was carved out of a hillside on the bay front and, as needed, the runway was extended eastward into the harbor by fill. The normal approach and landing was flown over the harbor straight into runway 31 from the east, and take-offs were made in the opposite direction. During a typical stormy period, because of the change in wind direction, the approach to landing had to be flown from over Chung Chao island to Stonecutter Island, then on a

curving right descending turn down between the apartment
buildings to the airport. The pilots loved it. To an
international airline pilot it was the ultimate challenge to
make a charlie-charlie approach and landing in nasty
weather, and casually stroll off the airplane.

The radio beacon on Cheung Chao transmits a Morse
code signal of CC (dah-dit-dah-dit, dah-dit-dah-dit). If your
receiver is properly tuned you will hear that Morse code
identifier and the needle on the cockpit indicator will point
to the station. In the International Aviation phonetic
alphabet a "C" is called charlie, hence the name charlie-
charlie. As Captain Dave Quinn describes it;

"Leave charlie-charlie at 1,000 feet and home on the
radio beacon on Stonecutter Island while descending to 600
feet. From there take up a heading of 043 degrees and
proceed visually, following the curving arc of strobes through
the city. Now look for the red and white checkerboard target
on a hillside and aim for it. Aim at the checkerboard until
you are concerned, hold it until you are terrified. Then make
a smart right turn to final and down between the apartment
buildings. This technique gives you a semblance of a final
approach and a chance to evaluate the perennial crosswind
from the left."

With typical British understatement the approach
instructions page notes "If visual contact is not achieved at
minimum altitude, an immediate missed approach must be
initiated; else terrain clearance will be lost"

The stewardesses hit Hong Kong like the invasion forces
on "D-Day". This was their ultimate shopping mall. Antiques,
tailoring, jewelry, cameras, it was all within a few blocks of
the hotel, and the merchants were happy to take their checks.
Some of them brought two suitcases, one empty, but to be
filled. I bought a few things, but my usual routine was to
take the Star Ferry to Hong Kong Island, walk a few blocks,
and board the tram to the top of the peak above the city.

There were some restaurants there, and a magnificent view of the harbor, and beyond into Mainland China.

PAA had a large maintenance base at Kai-Tak, primarily because labor was cheap. Overnight, a crew of Chinese workers could polish the entire exterior of a DC-4 airplane, and scrub the interior. The Chief Mechanic, Ed Lew, was a Chinese-American from California, and he ran a mechanic training program that became a model for airlines all over the Orient. Later, when the airplane entered the U.S.A. again, the company had to pay a duty assessment based on the value of the work performed on the airplane.

SHANGHAI

For a brief time we served Shanghai, until the Red Army forces took over the city. We stayed at the very nice "Cathay Hotel" along the "Bund", (the river front), and just signed for our meals and the company paid for them. The food was fabulous, and we were hard pressed to eat everything we ordered. I usually ordered a dinner of river shrimp cocktail, filet mignon, petit pois, baked potato, and always a Baked Alaska for dessert. Chinese currency generated by ticket sales could not be converted to US dollars, so we helped the company spend them. As the Mao-ist forces closed in on Shanghai the local currency became worthless. I still have a stack of $50,000 bills that are nothing but souvenirs. I bought a beautiful carved wooden statue of the Chinese god of antiquity in a back alley store for a twenty dollar bill and carefully carried it home as a gift for grandmother Antoinette. Off the hotel lobby was an antique shop, and I had admired a chess set in the window. The chess board was of inlaid wood, about 3 feet square, and the pieces were of carved white and green jade, but the price was $900, well out of my reach. On my last stopover, as the red forces were in artillery range of the city, the merchant saw me in the lobby and offered me the set for $200 "green", or American dollars. Unfortunately I only had about $40 in my pocket, there was no way to cash a check, and nobody else in the crew had enough money to make the buy. I suppose he buried the set somewhere and waited for the war to end.

A few days later I was on the last Pan American flight in and out of Shanghai. The invading army had captured one side of the airport, so to avoid flying directly over them we landed on the crosswind runway. With a 20-knot crosswind Roy Jenkins made a perfect landing, we shut down the left engines, boarded the company ground staff, and restarted the engines as we taxied out. The Red Chinese either chose not to fire at us as we took off, or they missed.

BANGKOK

Bangkok was a delight, as it seemed a small city of simple, happy people. The colors, the temples, and the food were a pleasure. Our layover hotel, the Ratanakasindr, was a six-story affair on the edge of town, with a serious drawback. The city water pressure was so low that the only way to get water to the upper floors was with an electric pump. At some time during the day the pump was turned on for a brief time, and the maids filled a five-foot high clay pot in each bathroom with water. The idea was that you used a dipper to bathe. One warm afternoon B.B.(Buckshot) Lien soaped himself down and decided to slide into the clay pot for a rinse. He managed this all right, but with the suds gone, found he could not get out. When he called for help, three members of his crew in adjacent rooms responded and, after consideration, decided to take the problem downstairs. The hotel was "hollow", that is all the rooms were on the outside and, in addition to a temperamental elevator, there was an inside circular ramp from the lobby to the sixth floor. They tipped Buckshot, and his clay pot, on his side and rolled him down the ramp to the lobby, where the clay pot hit the wall and broke into pieces, freeing him. With great dignity he stood up and strode, naked, back up the circular ramp to his room!

With a service frequency of only twice a week the crews had a three or four day layover in each direction. We had the use of the Bangkok Sports Club, with a comforting pool and an adequate restaurant. And we had access to the Bangkok Country club. That's where I learned about floating golf balls. Being slightly lighter than normal balls, they would just barely float in the numerous canals (klongs) that lined the fairways, and the lightly clad Klong boy we hired could retrieve them. So the game was played with a caddy, a klong boy, and usually a "forecaddie" to track our wayward tee shots. All this for a few American dollars. For a couple of dollars a day we could hire a Sarmala boy and his three-wheeled bicycle for transportation around the city. On a three, or four-day layover, each crewmember hired a boy for those days, and they waited in front of the hotel for our pleasure. I always hired the same one, Charlie, and for the length of our stay he was available twenty-four hours a day. I don't know how he did it but he was always wearing freshly washed and pressed shorts and shirt, and a huge smile. I always brought him some trinkets from Hong Kong, which made a big hit. In those early years Bangkok was still a quiet city, so it was quite a scene when six or seven of us charged off in Sarmalas to a restaurant for dinner, with bets being placed on the first one to reach the restaurant. In addition to the wonderful silk fabrics, knowledgeable shoppers could find bargains in gemstones and silver goods. I bought my father a silver-mounted tiger skull ashtray, but my step-mother wouldn't allow it in the house, so he kept it on his office desk.

CALCUTTA

Calcutta was the most depressing place I have ever seen. Our DC-4 arrived in Calcutta about the same time as the Constellation from New York, and both crews stayed overnight in the Staff House, and set out the next day on their return journeys. Our quarters were surrounded with broken-glass encrusted high walls, and security guards. We were cautioned about beggars, con artists, pickpockets, and just about every low life you can imagine. If you took a walk beyond the gate a man who could tell you all sorts of things about your life would probably accost you. (He bribed the desk clerk for a peek at your passport) Then there was the lady beggar holding a dead baby. She got a new dead baby every month or so. The only sightseeing venture we found was the Burning Ghat. The dead were ceremoniously carried to a riverside area, and incinerated with sandalwood and incense. When the ashes had cooled, the high priest carried a handful to the banks of the Ganges, wet them, and spread them on his naked body. We knew he was pure because there was a five inch spike, crosswise through his penis. He charged a rupee to allow a photograph.

THE EXPERIMENT

About that time the Chief Pilot in San Francisco decided that it would be a good idea to keep cockpit crews together to encourage a teamwork concept. The Air Corps had used this idea very effectively with the bomber crews during the war to heighten morale. I was teamed with Captain Steve Bancroft and Co-pilot Jack Kenny. Most of the time Stan Pierce was the Navigator. Steve and Jack were two of the most colorful characters in the entire airline, as well as two of the biggest troublemakers. The stories about Steve were a legend at Pan American, and I think most of them were true. He could out drink and outfight anyone, but he was also one of the nicest, warmest people I have ever known. The ladies adored him, as did Generals, Admirals, Ambassadors, and Movie stars. For a brief time he was married to Mae Clark, one of the cinema stars of the 1930s. He was also a very good pilot, which probably kept him from being fired after some of his off duty escapades. As a member of his crew I had the added duty of carrying his gin box. This was a small wicker case, custom made to carry two bottles of gin, a small bottle of Vermouth, olives, toothpicks, four glasses, and a container of ice. It was my job to keep it supplied and ready at all times. Steve and Jack would usually mix a martini in the cab on the way to our layover hotel. The Chief Pilot assigned me to that crew because I was rather quiet, and sober, and not apt to encourage them. Captain Bancroft called me Kid, or sometimes Tom-Tom, but always respected my opinions on aircraft airworthiness and maintenance. After about four months the experiment was abandoned, and we went back to random crew assignments. The problem was that a fixed three-man crew developed its own procedures, and when one of them was off on medical or vacation, the replacement man might have trouble adjusting to their ways. It was the best argument in the world for standardized cockpit procedures, and they were rapidly established.

To pass the time Steve told many stories on those long flights, most of which are very faint in my memory, but a few I remember.

Steve loved to sail, kept a boat in Sausalito, and knew the waters around the bay very well. In 1942, as their B314 neared San Francisco, they were advised that all of the bay area was below minimum ceiling conditions due to dense fog. The normal alternate landing site at Clear Lake was also reporting only a 100-foot ceiling. Pan American suggested his best alternate was at San Pedro, near Long Beach, so from overhead San Francisco Steve turned south, following where he thought the coast line would be. About thirty miles south of San Francisco he found what he was looking for, a break in the clouds. Through the opening in the fog he recognized Half Moon Bay on the California coast. He quickly descended through the opening and leveled the big Boeing about 100 feet above the water on a northerly heading. Staying a half-mile off the coast, Steve told the co-pilot to keep a sharp eye for a buoy with a number painted on it. At the end of a long ten minutes the co-pilot reported sighting a buoy, then called out the number "2". Steve knew that this was the first buoy marking the right side of the ship channel leading into the bay. He turned toward where he thought the bay would be and they watched for the number "4" buoy. A few minutes later that sighting confirmed their course and they followed the other buoys into the Golden

Gate. Only 100 feet above the bay waters, they were still dodging fog as they spotted the bottom of the south tower of the bridge. Now down to fifty feet, Steve chose to fly through the narrow space between the San Francisco anchorage and the south tower. He was afraid that he might meet a tanker in the mist under the middle of the bridge.

And there was his story about the Fourth of July in Bangkok. On this momentous holiday American Embassies all over the world do their best to fly the flag and entertain. Steve and his crew were in Bangkok on a westbound layover, and the American Ambassador, an old friend, suggested he bring his crew, in uniform, to the afternoon reception at the Embassy. Steve made the mistake of also bringing the Captain of the eastbound crew along, they being old friends. A while after arriving at the party the Ambassador took Steve aside to complain about that other Captain. He had obviously taken too many martinis from the waiter's trays, and now he had the Russian Ambassador in a corner. His strong language and finger emphasis were about to create an incident. Steve gathered the members of his crew, explained the problem, and proposed an action. They all surrounded the offender and while Steve whispered in his ear they moved him away from the grateful Russian. Suddenly the tipsy Captain called for a cab and left for the hotel. The rest of the crew were baffled by the sudden departure, and asked Steve to explain it. He said that he just bull-shitted the guy in his ear, but at the same time peed in his pants pocket. The poor soul thought he did it.

The postwar years brought some fantastic tourism for the crewmembers, but it also brought hardships. Most trips to the Orient entailed 20 to 23 days away from home, with lengthy layovers in some places. True, this was followed by perhaps two weeks off, but it was hard on family life.

With the end of hostilities and discharge from the Navy some of the Rocket Rangers left the airline and went on to other careers. Only about two thirds of the group stayed on with the airline. The lengthy Rocket Ranger training program shut down in the fall of 1943 when the demand for Engineers had been met. Several years after the end of the war the occasional need for more Flight Engineers was met by the old system of bringing in qualified people from the maintenance shops. In going over some old seniority lists I have determined that about 40 men entered the training program during a period of less than a year. Of that number 24 stayed on to retirement.

But the postwar years brought something really startling; stewardesses!

STEWARDESSES

Hope Parkinson

The company hired the first stewardesses in Miami in 1944, and we had heard rumors in San Francisco that they were considering doing the same in the Pacific region.

Imagine my surprise in 1948 when I met the first one and realized I had known her for years. Hope Parkinson was a close friend and schoolmate of my cousin, Marny Say, in Sacramento. She spent a week every summer as a guest at my grandmother Kewins summer cabin at Twain Harte in the Sierras, east of Sonora, California. We rode horseback, swam and fished together, and became close friends while teen-agers. And now this beautiful girl was the first stewardess to fly across the Pacific. Hope had been hired and trained in Miami in 1944, and flown out of Miami, New Orleans, and Brownsville for four years. While home in Sacramento for a vacation, she stopped at the Flight Service office at San Francisco to check on those same rumors. Roy Donham, head of the department, told her that the decision had just been made to start interviewing. When Hope told him that she would like to transfer to San Francisco Roy immediately called Miami, and she moved west the next month. In a few years she became the Stewardess Coordinator, and the leading public relations figure for the airline. Her Irish smile appeared in hundreds of press releases, magazines, and foreign newspapers. *Charm* magazine did a feature article on her, and she was part of the crew on almost every inaugural flight. Hope was a member of the team of Flight Service personnel who helped design the galley for the Pan American B-377 Stratocruiser. Needless to say, she was very busy, but I managed to take up some of her time.

In 1949 a wealthy Indian gentleman went to the Mayo Clinic for treatment. After a few months there he was discharged, and told to go home, as they had done all they could for him. In his weakened condition, he asked PanAm if they could provide a traveling companion to help him through the long DC-4 journey back to Calcutta. Hope agreed to the assignment.

She sat next to him all the way to Calcutta. Because of his frail condition it was necessary to overnight where possible, so she helped him on and off the airplane, and in and out of taxis and hotels. It required a week of travel to get him home, but she took care of his dietary needs on and off the airplane, and even took care of his laundry, and talked to him all the way. By the time she delivered him to his waiting family, he thought she was the most wonderful person in the world. Of course, he had to pay PanAm for her round trip ticket.

A few months later, when she arrived from a trip, I met Hope at the airport to drive her to her apartment on Sacramento Street in San Francisco. While I waited in my car she stopped at the Flight Service office to pick up her mail and turn in some reports. The secretary gave her a small package, and said that an Indian gentleman had stopped in a few days earlier to leave it for "Miss Hope". He said his father had recently died, and had asked that the next member of his family passing through San Francisco carry the package to the Pan American office. Hope opened the package when she got to my car and found nine matched rubies, packed in a layer of cotton. In San Francisco we stopped on Sutter Street to see a friend of mine, who was a wholesale jeweler. He was stunned, and said they were very valuable. The next day Hope took them back to the airport and turned them over to her boss, because employees were not allowed to accept any kind of gratuity, especially one of such value. A few months later Roy gave them back to her because the company could find no way of locating the donor. She eased her conscience by having my jeweler friend mount them on a platinum cross, which Hope gave to her god-daughter.

In the summer we drove to the Twain Harte cabin to spend a few days with my grandmother Antoinette, and my father and stepmother. My father fell helplessly in love with her, and Antoinette was thrilled, as Hope had always been one of her summer favorites. Antoinette had hopes that we would marry, and so did I. Later that year my parents and grandmother decided to fly to Honolulu for a week's vacation at the Halekulani Hotel, and Hope and I arranged to be on the crew in both directions.

While we did not try to keep our romance a secret, we did keep a very low profile. When asked, we just said we were old family friends.

Hope told me that she was being bothered by one of the Captains at the San Francisco base. He had started calling her several times a week, asking her to join him for lunch or for a drive in the country. She always found a way to decline gracefully. In addition to not really liking him very much, it bothered her that he was married. One late afternoon we were having a glass of wine in her apartment, and talking about where we should go for dinner, when the telephone rang. Hope said that she was sure it would be Bob. I answered the phone.

"Uh, hello, is Miss Parkinson in?" I recognized the voice.

"Yes, just a minute". I put the phone down, then picked it up again and said;

"I'm sorry, she just stepped into the tub. Can I take a message?"

"Uh, no, I'll call another time."

"I'll tell her you called, Bob". I hung up. I could visualize the thoughts running through his mind;

"Who the hell was that? He knows my name!" He never called again.

DELHI BELLY

The airline was made up of three divisions; Pacific—Alaska, Atlantic, and Latin American, and each division was almost a separate airline. When the Ivory Tower in New York decided that the Constellation service from New York to Calcutta should be extended as far as Hong Kong, it made sense. The Chinese greatly admired the Constellation because of its triple rudder tail, (something about dragons), and they were fast becoming very big airline customers. But the route from New Delhi to Hong Kong belonged to the Pacific division so that sector would have to be, inconveniently, flown by Pacific crews. With one day's notice I was whisked off to LaGuardia for a six-week training course on the Constellation, and a check ride to London and back. The next day by United to San Francisco, and the following day I deadheaded to Hong Kong. This was before "Jet lag", but I was pretty numb when I reached the Peninsula Hotel in Hong Kong. The next day I operated the Constellation to Bangkok, Calcutta, and on to New Delhi for a three-day layover at the Swiss Hotel. Then back by the same route to Hong Kong for a two-day layover. I was supposed to do this for three weeks, but it being November and December, my potential replacements had all reached their flying hours limit for the year. Every time I returned to Hong Kong I asked hopefully if my replacement had arrived. My wires to

San Francisco crew scheduling were futile as there was no one available until the first of January.

In spite of my best efforts I came down with diarrhea on every stopover in New Delhi. I brought canned food from Hong Kong, brushed my teeth in grapefruit juice, and only ordered hardboiled eggs, dry toast, and coffee at breakfast, but I must have been diarrhea prone. Some found safety in curry, the hotter the better, but I just cannot handle hot food. I was not alone, as many of the crew shared the misery. Fortunately the lavatories on the Constellation were at the forward end of the cabin. My stomach healed in Hong Kong, but rebelled again as soon as I returned to New Delhi

The flying time for this route was about 14 hours, and the time on duty was more than 18 hours. The FAA had not yet established firm maximums, and the unions were still organizing, so we just did it. To make matters worse, on the eastbound trip from Bangkok to Hong Kong, the early morning winter weather was frequently below our 1,000' ceilings for the radio range approach, so we would have to divert to Manila for fuel, and wait for the weather to improve. Our subsequent arrival at the lobby of the Peninsula Hotel did not speak very well for the image of Pan American. With a 24-hour beard, badly wrinkled uniform, and feet dragging slowly up the front steps we were not an example of PanAm's finest. We looked like we had been "worked hard and put away wet".

For 62 days I alternated between diarrhea in New Delhi and constipation in Hong Kong, and lost 15 pounds from my already skinny frame. At last, in early January, my replacement arrived and I deadheaded home. The next day I went into the Chief's office with fire in my eyes. He tried, very sympathetically, to explain what happened but I was still mad. Then he made a telephone call and told me that Captain Gray wanted to see me. Harold Gray was then Chief Pilot in San Francisco, and was one day to become head of the airline as Trippe's chosen successor. He was respected, even admired, by everyone in the airline industry. I sat in his office and drank a cup of coffee while he went through the same tale. The only alternative was to leave me there for two months, or cancel trips. Then he said that he had told crew scheduling that I was off for thirty days, handed me two roundtrip tickets to Acapulco, and a voucher for seven days at the Las Americas hotel. I decided not to quit yet.

Fortunately, Hope was on vacation for the month of January, and she joined me to Acapulco, along with a couple from Sacramento. The tourists had not discovered Acapulco yet, and it was still a nice, small resort town. The hotel was not air-conditioned but, as it was located on a cliff above the bay, there was usually a good sea breeze. Our evening meals were on the terrace under the stars while a dance band played. We started the day at the "Morning Beach" and spent the afternoons by the hotel pool, with some water skiing and deep-sea fishing thrown in. When the wonderful week ended we returned on the Aeronaves de Mexico DC-3 to Mexico City and then by Mexicana DC-4 to San Francisco.

On our return I made reservations for the two of us at the Tahoe Tavern for the grand opening of Squaw Valley ski resort. The resort had no overnight accommodations as yet, so the old hotel on the north shore had agreed, for the first time in its long history, to stay open to accommodate skiers. On Saturday night a great formal dinner was held to celebrate the opening, and several hundred people, most of them from Hollywood, arrived for it. For additional hype the Hollywood actress and dancer, Ann Miller, was Miss Squaw Valley and she put on a convincing performance, dancing in an Indian squaw costume. When Hope and I made reservations for dinner we discovered that it was a formal affair, and we were not equipped for it. With nothing but after-ski clothes, we were shuffled to a card table in a back corner of the dining room. Wayne and Sandy Poulson also arrived in after-ski attire, and they joined us. I had known

Wayne since my college days when we frequently competed in Inter-collegiate ski events. and both Hope and I knew him as a fellow PanAm crew member. He had discovered Squaw Valley, and purchased it, but lacked the funds to see it developed properly. In time he called Alex Cushing, an eastern developer and skier. Alex came, saw, and was sold. He went on to start the Squaw Valley Corporation, bring in some eastern financing, and develop the resort. In return for the land in the west end of the valley, and the Forest Service leases, Wayne received 5% of the Corporation, but held on to the rest of the valley. During the long evening affair, Cushing introduced almost everyone in the room; the contractor who did the paving, the sewer contractor, the surveyor, but not Wayne. Wayne was viewed as a competitor and a thorn in the Corporation's side. But we enjoyed our evening together, and the next day Wayne gave us a skiing tour of the few trails that had been developed. On our way back to San Francisco we stopped for a few days in Sacramento at the Parkinson home on the banks of the Sacramento River, and I had time to get to know Dorothy Parkinson, Hopes widowed mother. We got along very well, and I felt that she approved of me.

So I recuperated from that 62 days of agony in a grand style, and went back for another session in Hong Kong and Delhi. This time the company Flight Surgeon provide me with a small medicine kit, which was helpful. And they promised that I would only be gone for three weeks.

STRATOCRUISER

During the last year of the war the Boeing Airplane Company started planning for post-war projects. The B-29 "Superfortress" was a very successful design, and provided a wing that could be adapted to a transport airplane readily. Pratt & Whitney had a new 3500 H.P. engine available, and design work was begun. In 1948 the first B-377 aircraft were delivered to Pan American and service started from San Francisco to Honolulu and from New York to London. The airplane was a huge success with the public as it represented the ultimate in luxury. The downstairs lounge, large berths, and speed put Pan Am far ahead of the competition for a short while, but at a cost. The airplane was expensive to operate and maintain, and for the first few years the big engine was very temperamental. With four rows of 7 cylinder radial sections the P & W 4360 engine was the most powerful aircraft engine ever built, and the most complicated. Hundreds of moving parts, 56 spark plugs prone to fouling, and seven magnetos all added up to potential maintenance problems. We called it the "corncob" because that is what it looked like.

The flight deck was huge and was like a sunroom. There were 13 pieces of multi-layer glass in the windshield, and on a bright westbound afternoon flight the glare was blinding. One of the Captains suggested the company should supply the cockpit crew with Ray-bans, and the Chief Pilot said;

"Show me a pilot who doesn't already have some Ray-bans, and I will buy some for him".

The Engineer's station was set on a pedestal in the middle of the flight deck, just behind the center console between the pilots. His main instrument panel rose on the right side and overhead, with the engine controls just aft of the pilot's center console. The flight deck was so wide that access to the pilot's seats was from the outside. Behind the Captains seat was a seat for an observer, and behind that an upper and lower berth for crew rest. Tucked away in the aft rear corner was the navigator's table, with a small instrument panel.

One of the quirks of the radial engine is that when it is at rest a little oil may ooze down the cylinder walls of the lower cylinders, past the piston rings and into the combustion chamber. This is particularly true when the cylinders and rings have worn a bit. Engine performance is not affected by this wear, but it does provide some entertainment. As that engine starts the tablespoon of oil in each lower cylinder creates an enormous cloud of smoke. The smoke dissipates in a few seconds, but it is impressive, and the crew could usually estimate the number of hours since overhaul on that engine by the amount of smoke.

The Stratocruiser was a stable airplane in most respects, but in turbulent conditions it could be uncomfortable. Not for the passengers, their part of the airplane was fine—but for the attendant in that galley back in the tail area it could be brutal. In rough air it was almost impossible to stand in the galley, and they usually had no choice but to suspend meal service, and take a seat.

On a clear quiet day the trip from San Francisco to Honolulu was the ultimate in luxury and confidence. All was right with the world. But we had heard stories for years about a problem Captain Lanier Turner had on one of those perfect days. In 1991 at a convention of the old pilots in Seattle they persuaded Lanier to tell his story to 350 of us.

About halfway to Honolulu on one of those perfect days, Lanier decided to do his usual public relations walk through the cabin. He put on his coat and cap and stepped through the cockpit door into the cabin. Lanier was a handsome man, every inch a Captain, and he felt very comfortable as he stepped into the forward aisle of the cabin. On either side of the forward cabin was a lavatory. No "men" or "women" signs, it was first come first served, with a locking door feature. Neither door indicated occupancy so Lanier stepped into the one on the right side, headfirst. Those doors were unusual in that they were a pair of folding doors. On each pair of door panels a center hinge allowed the doors to fold inward. The oriental lady occupying the lavatory probably couldn't read the signs about locking the doors, and was very distressed when Lanier made his entrance. She screamed and pushed against the doors, trapping his neck and knocking off his cap. Lanier tried to pry the doors open so as to release their grip on his neck, but she had a mechanical advantage over his efforts and now braced her feet against the doors and started pounding his head with her leather purse. In his struggles Lanier's feet slipped, and as he fell to the floor his feet became trapped by the lavatory doors on the other side of the aisle. One of the flight attendants finally came to his rescue and he retreated to the flight deck to compose himself. Lanier admitted it was probably one of the low points of his airline career.

Worlin "Wug" Gray was one of the ex-military pilots hired just after the end of the war, and being in the lower reaches of the seniority list was serving as a Second Officer, or Navigator. He not only had a great sense of humor but a wonderful talent as an "Aviators Poet". I suppose the long hours sitting at the navigation table offered him the chance to scribble some thoughts in rhyme. In particular I remember "The Nude Nymph on Number Three", and "The Legendary Lien Patrol". Editor Jack Laird published some of his best efforts in the bi-monthly "Clipper" newspaper. "Wug" also found good use for his talents in his navigation tasks.

The usual routine was for the Navigator to plot our position on his chart back there in the corner of the flight deck, compute a new magnetic heading, and relay it to the cockpit. He wrote it in one inch high letters on a small piece of paper, stuck a loop of masking tape on the back, and passed it to me for relay to the Co-pilot. The Co-pilot showed it to the Captain, and pasted it on the middle of the glare shield where both could see it. Then one of them would turn the knob on the autopilot control to bring the airplane to the new heading. On this occasion the two pilots were having a vigorous discussion about something, which had nothing to do with airplanes, and when I relayed the new heading slip to the Co-pilot he posted it and resumed the discussion. The poet watched his remote compass indicator to confirm the heading change, but nothing happened. He looked at me, and I shrugged my shoulders and gave him a yak-yak signal with my hand. After a few minutes went by, he pulled out a larger piece of paper, wrote a message, and handed it to me for relay. It got an immediate response, as the message said; "Stop picking your nose and shooting the breeze, you're off your heading by seven degrees".

Wug has given me permission to print his poem. In fact, he has all but insisted on it.

THE NUDE NYMPH ON NUMBER THREE

*When just a copilot, young and free
a-flying an aircraft across the sea,
a nude nymph I did chance to see
basking on the nacelle of number three*

*The gauges all were within the law
Yet I knew this maid I saw,
This streamlined lovely in the raw
Should cause at least a little yaw.*

For fear the phantom should disappear
I warily woke the engineer.
By his lecherous, lewd and lascivious leer
I knew to him the thing was clear.

With the vile lust which is engineer's trait
The wretched rogue rushed at such a rate
That he "bopped" his head on the defroster plate
And collapsed to the floor in an unconscious state.

The stewardess surely should be shown
this nude nymph out there all alone.
So as on the azure air we drone
I called her on the interphone.

"Tell me lass, what dos't thou see
through the glass just to the right of thee?"
And she said back, as bored as could be
"Just a nude nymph on number three.

Now the engineer rose from his unconscious state
And did grin a ghastly glowering gape,
Until his cranium contacted the defroster plate
And he fell to the floor, where he had been of late.

Seeing the engineer on the deck dispensed
And the disgusted stewardess's countenance
The captain came up to view events,
The very essence of regal elegance.

He slightly swooned, the sight to see
And reverently blessed his seniority,
And searched the manual frantically
For what's done 'bout a nymph on number three.

The ruckus so my attention drew
I noticed not where we flew.
And the next thing we knew
We were bouncing and bumping through a big Cu.

We broke right out as quick as could be
And all looked out expectantly.
Our horrified eyes could readily see
There was no nude nymph on number three.

Of course the question never dies;
Who is this maid who haunts the skies?
Flew we o'er the depths where an aircraft lies
And she from her watery grave did rise?

Perhaps a stewardess from heaven or hell
Who was wont to ride our wing a spell,
And recall the days before foul fate fell,
and swept her to her present knell.

Could be a "beanie" with kids at home
Whose soul can't rest once it's known.
The great wide sky and motors drone
And in some foreign city, longs to roam.

Some say such a thing could not be
But a fleeting figment of fantasy.
Ah! But brother you know when you see
A nude nymph on number three.

Captain Worlin U Gray
Pan American World Airways
1948

ATLANTIC DIVISION

My transfer to New York was typical of the Inhale-Exhale woes of airline employment. The Boeing Stratocruiser, which replaced the Douglas DC-4, could carry twice the load and fly much faster. Where there had been three flights a day to Honolulu now there were two. The new airliners speed meant that they could do more trips in the same time so even fewer crews were needed. It seemed to be something of a five-year cycle of hiring, furlough, recall, then hiring again to start another cycle. It was two steps forward followed by one step back. The problem did not seem to affect the Flight Attendants or the Maintenance Department, only the cockpit staff. I was on the ragged edge of being furloughed (laid off), but managed to squeeze into New York in the fall of 1950, near the bottom of the seniority list.

That put me at a 3,000-mile disadvantage in my pursuit of Hope Parkinson, but In March of 1952 she came to New York to visit me. She told her family and friends that she was going to Bermuda for a short vacation, but we spent five days refreshing our romance and talking about the future. We were both ready to tie the knot but I had just returned from a month-long skiing vacation in Austria, and could not obtain any more time off. We decided to marry quietly in New York and work it out from there. We declared our vows in an Episcopal Church in Great Neck, New York, with the Rector's wife and my friend James Chadwick in attendance.

After a two-day honeymoon Hope went back to California to give the company notice and ship her belongings east. I went out on a ten-day trip to Africa, and came home to start house hunting. A month later we settled in a rental house in Levittown, Long Island and started to look for a home to buy. In a similar fashion, many of the young pilots and engineers found wives in the aircraft cabin. We soon formed a close social group, as many of us felt like refugees from California.

It is hard to explain just how vital our relationships with the other crewmembers became. When I was gone on a ten-day trip to Johannesburg, Hope was involved in an automobile accident and, although she only had some bruises, our baby son suffered a broken leg. Two days later, on my arrival at LaGuardia, one of the other Engineers was waiting in the Customs area to break the news to me and give me a lift home. Our son George was in a full lower body cast, weighing about twenty pounds, and Hope had one arm in a sling. She had made a sled out of a piece of cardboard and some cord, and for two days she had been towing him behind her around the house. Some of the other airline wives were dropping in every day to help and some brought prepared meals. I have always considered my co-workers and their families to be part of my own extended family, because every one of them was ready to help on any occasion, and after all these years they still are. In my group of close friends, numbering about 100, I can recall only two divorces.

I always felt that the biggest advantage of my job was that when I came home from a trip, the only thing I carried was my luggage. I left the job at the airport, and seldom thought about it again until it was time to go on another trip. For a few days, or perhaps a week, my full attention was on my family and my home, a life-style that I would recommend to anyone who wishes to stay married.

LOCKHEED
CONSTELLATION

In early June of 1951, while based in New York, I was on a Lockheed Constellation trip to Stockholm, when we had a precarious return flight. Out of Keflavik, Iceland, bound for Gander, Newfoundland, we had a cockpit full of check pilots. The American Overseas Airline (AOA) merger had just been completed, and all those office types were being "exposed" to the AOA northern European routes to Keflavik, Oslo, Stockholm and Helsinki. The aircraft, N88837, was a bit weary, and between Keflavik, Iceland and Gander, Newfoundland we shut down number 2 engine because of an exhaust valve failure on No. 9 cylinder. When the engine suddenly started running rough, a quick scan of the new "Lindburg Analyzer" showed both spark plugs on that cylinder shorted. We feathered it immediately, before the broken exhaust valve pounded a hole in the piston, and pressed on to Gander at 5,000 feet. As we neared the Newfoundland coast we learned that every airport in that area was closed by weather. Over Gander Airport number 4 engine packed it in due to a bearing failure on the right fuel injection pump. We feathered that engine's propeller too. At full power on the two remaining engines we were down to 1,000 feet, and still descending, hoping for Boston.

Captain Jooge Warren, in the co-pilot's seat, saw the runway lights at Stephenville Air Force base through a thin spot in the clouds. He grabbed the controls, closed the throttles, and dove through the hole and landed. We did not even have time to call the tower. A few hours later, a Stratocruiser landed and picked up the passengers and extra crew, leaving a Captain, Copilot, and myself with the Constellation. I called New York and told them that I needed a new cylinder assembly and two injection pumps. The parts arrived the next day on the local airline, but no mechanics. I spent the next two days at the airport, managed to borrow engine stands and tools from the Air Force, and hired two off-duty Air Force mechanics for five dollars an hour. When the airplane was ready we did a short test flight. After landing I said I would fuel the airplane and we could get the hell out of there. The Captain and Copilot had spent some of their time at the Officers club, and the Captain said; "No, we need a few hours for this corporal (bartender at the Officers Club) to go out in a boat and pull his lobster traps!" We took off a couple of hours later, with 98 live lobsters (at 25 cents apiece) in large cardboard Kotex cartons, laced with strands of seaweed.

Half an hour out of LaGuardia the No. I engine failed.

As I remember, we handed out lobsters in Customs, and I went to the Chief Flight Engineer's office to check in and pick up my mail. Jim Etchison, (the chief) gave me hell for spending two days fixing that airplane. He cooled down a bit when I informed him that they had neglected to send any mechanics, and that I had done the maintenance myself. Standing there with two large live lobsters in my hand as a gift I restrained myself and dropped them into an empty wastebasket, instead of on his lap. I got into my MG and went home to Garden City and had a great lobster feast with my neighbors.

As I think back on it, I just cannot believe how bad those engines were. In reviewing my log books I found that in two years I feathered 48 engines on the Constellations. In twelve years on the 707 I only shut down one, and in twelve years on the 747 I only shut down one.

Flight operations in the Atlantic were a big change from what I had known in the Pacific. Winter weather was often miserable in New York and northern Europe, with In-flight icing, slippery runways, and frequent instrument approaches. I often felt that I was working for a different airline, because I did not know very many of the people I worked with, and all of the layover cities were new to me. Even the uniforms were different, because in winter we put black covers on our uniform caps and for the first time in my life I bought an overcoat and galoshes. On the plus side there was a whole new part of the world to see, and I wanted to see as much of it as I could.

During the first few months I was assigned to the African route and got a good view of Portugal and Africa. Lisbon is a very colorful city where we usually had a two or three day layover. It has many historical sites, well preserved, and conveniently compact. Growing up in the San Joaquin Valley of California I had known many Portuguese immigrants, and was familiar with their festivals and food, so I felt very comfortable walking the hilly streets of Lisbon, and eating at small waterfront restaurants. From Lisbon the schedule to Johannesburg was an agonizing 28 or 29 hours of flying time via Dakar, Senegal; Monrovia, Liberia; Accra, Ghana; and Leopoldville, Belgian Congo (later Kinshasa, Zaire, and now the Democratic Congo Republic). Duty time was 34 or 35 hours for the double crew, and often longer because of mechanical delays. When an engine broke down, the Engineer took off his uniform, put on borrowed coveralls, and picked up a wrench. The cabin attendants had a layover in Accra, but the Pilots and Engineers gritted their teeth and went all the way.

We had several days rest in Johannesburg before retracing the route back to Lisbon, and we sorely needed them. The crews had access to the Wanderers Club and its golf course, swimming pool and dining room, so I started taking golf lessons. A day trip to the capital city of Pretoria was worthwhile, or a tour of one of the deep gold mines. The more adventurous ones went on a guided tour to Kruger Park.

From Lisbon we also operated to Barcelona and either Nice or Marseille where we had lunch, and then returned to Lisbon. On the stopover in Nice the restaurant in the terminal building always had a large table reserved for the crew next to a picture window over the ramp area. In addition to the lovely lunch of veal, or chicken, and a Nicoise salad, there would be a glass with a Coca Cola logo at every setting. It looked like Coke, but it was red wine.

To me the worst trip was the dreary one to South America. After a one night stopover in San Juan, we went to Caracas, Venezuela, and then on to Belem, Brazil for a few days at the old Grande Hotel. Close to the steamy mouth of the Amazon, Belem had few things to offer aside from the old Opera House, (a remnant of the "Rubber Days"), and the Amazon Bar off the lobby of the hotel. The bar was one of the only air-conditioned places in Belem, but did not open until 6 p.m., and we were usually waiting when the door opened. Inside the door was a life sized carved wooden statue of a female Amazon warrior whose right breast had been amputated so as not to interfere with a bowstring.

During dinner in the hotel dining room, a five-piece orchestra performed, and I still have a vision of the balding chubby violin player, wearing an old tuxedo and drenched in sweat. As the temperature cooled in the evening it was nice to sit on the terrace in front of the hotel and enjoy a Cafezino, a small cup of paint stripping coffee, while watching the evening Paseo—the young girls walking slowly in groups, talking and giggling, as the young men swaggered and postured. The older couples watched closely while talking with friends. Down the street a few blocks was a movie theater, where for ten cents you could sit on a wooden bench and watch an old flickering movie.

Rio de Janeiro was an interesting city for a different reason. Sited on a magnificent harbor, Rio is the heart of Brazil. The Copacabana beach in front of our hotel was glorious (but infested with sand fleas) and the city was colorful and filled with music. But only a few blocks away were miserable shanties built on the hillsides and filled with desperately poor people. The whole economy seemed to be built on a system whereby everyone earned their living by doing their neighbor's laundry. After a few trips to South America I found it depressing and requested assignment to European trips.

RAINBOW CLASS

In 1953, shortly after Hope and I were married, the Douglas Aircraft Company started delivering the new DC-6B aircraft to Pan American, and this was just what Juan Trippe had been waiting for. The company broke the mold and inaugurated what was called Rainbow Class flights from New York to Europe with the new aircraft, while the Boeing Stratocruisers continued to provide the President Special first class service across the Atlantic. With these first discount fares to London, Frankfurt, Paris, and Rome, and a strong dollar, working Americans could easily afford that European vacation, and it changed the airline industry. The company bought more than 40 of the Douglas aircraft, and the Constellations soon disappeared. The Pratt and Whitney 2800 engine used on the DC-6B was an excellent workhorse with outstanding reliability, and soon the on-time performance was at an all-time high, as was the Pan American stock price.

The layovers in some of the great cities of Europe were a golden opportunity, and Hope helped me make the most of it. In 1950 with two stewardess friends, Betty Fitzgerald and Sally Breuner, Hope had done an intense 30-day tour of the major cities of Europe and she had made a daily log of their travels and impressions. Before every trip we dug into her diaries, our encyclopedias, and the public library for information and history, so that I was prepared for each layover. There was not much available as yet in the way of tours in that area so I walked. An eight-mile stroll through London, or Paris, or Rome, was a real pleasure, even in the rain, and I soon learned my way through the subways and on the busses. Lunch in a British pub, a French café, a German ratskeller, or an Italian trattoria was always good, and they made me and my dollars feel welcome. Hope had a great-aunt south of London and I frequently visited her and her family. Her son, Rafe, was a second World War hero, having served very effectively as an underground agent in France, and was still a member of his reserve regiment. One evening I was his guest at the regimental dinner in the Tower of London. The traditional after-dinner passing of the port, and the toasts to the Queen were fascinating. Rafe had cautioned me that the regiment did not stand for the toasts, ever since Henry the Eighth, while dining in the same hall, had told them to remain seated, because "their loyalty was unquestioned."

As in most of the cities of Europe there is so much to see that it is hard to know where to start. Our London hotel, the Kensington Palace, was only a few blocks from several good museums and that was a good choice on a rainy day. On a decent day I hopped a bus or subway and walked through a part of London. On a sunny day there are many great places along the Thames river, Windsor is a short bus ride away, and the changing of the Guard at Buckingham Palace is a great scene.

A few blocks from our hotel in Paris I found a wine shop where the proprietor spoke some English. I told him that I knew little about wine, and he was delighted to try to teach me. On each Paris layover, I bought 5 bottles of a wine he selected, and stored them in a small area of our cellar. We always opened one bottle shortly after my return, and took notes on our opinions of it.

Hemingway wrote, "Paris is a moveable feast". He said that once you have lived in Paris, it is a feast that you take with you wherever you go. With my brief visits I could not qualify for that blessing, but I did gain an appetite for some of the pleasures Paris offered. The parks, the boulevards, the people, all seemed so alive and joyful that it was infectious.

On the Left Bank (across the Seine) was a little restaurant called "Le Grenouille" (The green frog). The proprietor's name was Roger, pronounced "Rojay", and he was a one of a kind character. There was no waiting area and they did not take reservations, so you were told to stand amongst the diners while you waited for a vacancy at one of the long tables. The seated diners graciously offered a sip of their wine, a frog leg, a shred of lamb, or a taste of their goose to whet your appetite.

When space was open at a table, Roger would personally escort us. He always chose the youngest lady in our party to lead the way. That was frequently a new stewardess on her first trip to Paris. Roger put his left hand on her shoulder to guide her, and his right hand somewhere below her waist to help her along. The cheers and applause of the crowd drowned out her protests. The starter course was always a large platter of Frog Legs Provencale, followed by leg of lamb, roast duck, chicken, or braised beef. The standard dessert was an ice cream dish, but with a twist. The waiter brought a dish with two round scoops of ice cream, and a tall cylinder of ice cream covered by a dollop of strawberry syrup. When served to a lady the waiter stood, spoon in hand, waiting for her to bite the top off the spire. Then she was rewarded with the spoon to finish her dessert. Again, the crowd was watching, chanting, and cheering, and that young stewardess had a night she will never forget. After dinner Roger always walked out with us to say goodbye, and for a kiss on the cheek, the new stewardess won a small metal green frog as a souvenir. She was a long way from Iowa, and I was sure a long way from Modesto. The Parisians had such a joyful approach to life that I think it changed me. I didn't quite earn the Feast, but I sure liked the sample.

Frankfurt took a tremendous pounding during the last months of the war, and ten years later the damage was still very obvious. Whole blocks of the downtown area had been cleared of debris, and new construction was under way. A rather dark, dreary city, but in the evening, in a Bierstube, the world was bright and cheerful. Our usual routine was a good schnitzel dinner and a stop at Meyr Gustles' beer hall on the way back to the Metropol Hotel. The large Oom-Pa-Pa orchestra and the huge steins of beer were a good ending to an evening. If you were lucky—or unlucky, depending on your mood, you would be handed the baton and asked to conduct the next orchestral number. The band, of course, ignored your efforts and played the song just as they always did, and they thoroughly enjoyed the round of drinks that you provided.

If you have been to Rome, you will understand my dilemma. There is so much to see, and never enough time. I did not know where to start, so Hope suggested the Pantheon. A good choice, as it represents the multicultural history of ancient Rome. Standing under the large opening at the top of the huge dome, I wished I had a toga to wear.

The crews efficiently spread the word when someone found a special restaurant, and it was difficult to keep up with all the latest finds. They were all so good that you wanted to return for a second try. La Biblioteca was one we went to often. It offered excellent fresh seafood, and the best cannelloni in Rome. Douglas Fairbanks and Mary Pickford had endorsed Alfredo's long ago but we found it disappointing.

With the prevailing westerly winds the crew could make a fuel stop at Shannon and continue on to London, Frankfurt or Paris. However on the return trip the cabin crew could continue on to New York, but because of the new FAA

limitations the cockpit crew had to take a 24-hour rest stop
in Ireland. For years our layover facility was at the Old Ground
Hotel in Shannon. The hotel had a pleasant dining room,
and a most enjoyable bar. At first it puzzled me when all the
locals would disappear at seven p.m., as we went to dinner,
to be replaced half an hour later by a new group of merry
makers. Then I learned that under the "opening hours"
laws of that time, only a traveler could buy a drink after 7
P.M. So all the locals had walked a mile to the next village,
and half way there they passed a group coming in our
direction, making them all travelers.

The crews began to complain strongly about sanitary
conditions at the Old Ground Hotel. The station manager
investigated and agreed that it was bad, and promptly moved
us to a more modern hotel in nearby Limerick. Captain A.O.
Powell and I were among the first crews to stay at the new
hotel. Powell had recently taken up golf, so when we
checked in at the front desk he wanted to try the local course.
The co-pilot declined, but Powell and I got an early start
and took a taxi the 3 or 4 miles to the clubhouse. The course
was deserted, except for a greens-keeper pushing a mower
and an elderly lady in the clubhouse. We paid a few dollars
for greens fees and rental clubs, and started for the first tee.
The lady followed us out and asked, "would we be wanting
lunch?" That seemed a good idea so we agreed. "Would you
prefer lamb chops, pork chops, trout, or beefsteak?" We
chose the pork chops, chips (fried potatoes) and a salad,
and teed off. As we were working our way down the third
fairway we saw the good lady on her bicycle pedaling toward
Limerick. I asked Powell; "Where do you suppose she is
going?" He rightly guessed; "To Limerick, to buy some pork
chops?" I have recently learned that the Old Ground Hotel
has been rebuilt and is now a quality establishment. I would
like to visit it again.

In 1953 I was offered a position as a "Check Engineer"
on the DC-6B aircraft, and took the job because it paid 10%

more salary, but also because I could spend more time at home. With one young son, and another child on the way, the long trips had lost their appeal. Now I was teaching classes, giving check rides, and acting as a designated FAA license examiner. And I was staying close to home. We had bought a new home in Westbury, Long Island, only a half-hour drive from Idlewild airport (Now J.F. Kennedy). Our little neighborhood of California ranch style homes was a delight, with a wonderful mix of people and lots of young children. About a third of our neighbors were Jewish, and Hope and I began to get an education in their culture. We were included in their festivals and Bar Mitzvahs, and they were part of our evening volleyball games and cookouts. We enjoyed Westbury and our friends there, and our departure for California in 1955 was with a mixture of sorrow and joy. I am still in touch with some of those neighbors of fifty years ago. We had accumulated about fifty bottles of wine in that little cellar, and the moving company would not take it, so we held several wine tasting parties for our neighbors and Pan American friends. I put the last five bottles in the back of the new Ford Station Wagon with the dogs and the house plants and drove west, while a slightly pregnant Hope and our two young sons took TWA.

HOME AGAIN

After selling our Westbury home at a good profit, and coming home to California, I found myself at the junior end of the seniority list and flying on the Boeing Stratocruiser. Several months later the new DC-7C aircraft arrived, and because I had been a Check Engineer on the DC-7B when I left New York, I was offered an office job at San Francisco.

Even though I was qualified on the DC-7B aircraft, and was a Designated FAA Examiner on the aircraft, the office decided that I should take the full training course, as there were some minor differences between the "B" and "C" models. Bob Huettl, Jim Lowe, and I attended a five-week ground school class during which I spent part of the time correcting the misinformation the instructors had. They were all new to the aircraft, while I had been teaching and flying on a similar model for a year. There were no simulators as yet, so flight training was still done on a live aircraft in a four-hour session of take-offs, landings, and simulated in-flight emergencies. Then each student sat down in a cubicle with a Check Engineer for 5 days of oral examination. It was not so much an examination as it was an exhaustive review of the aircraft systems, limitations, and procedures. This was to be followed by a check ride to Honolulu and back.

There was an excellent company cafeteria at the San Francisco base, but we usually brought a bag lunch and used the break to review what we had learned in the morning classes. Our cubicles were on the third floor of the old Marine Air Terminal, and up a flight of stairs was the former Control Tower, now deserted. With a great view of the airport, it soon became our lunchroom. Hugh Gourdin was assigned to give me the "Check" exam, and Ralph Bareuthers and Jim Franklin were assigned to my classmates, Huettl and Lowe. On the first day, the five others opened their paper bag lunches and started on their peanut butter and jelly sandwiches and fruit. Hope had prepared lunch for me, and packed it in one of those little wicker hampers. There was a cold sliced chicken breast that had been cooked in a butter and wine sauce, an avocado to be sliced in half, a small container of Girard's dressing, and two soft rolls, with butter. The hamper was equipped with paper napkins, utensils, salt and pepper, and a small thermos of coffee.

The next day, as I enjoyed another superb lunch, I noticed that the other lunches had improved. Not a sign of peanut butter! That evening I told Hope that the other wives had been put on notice, and we both enjoyed a joke about it. On the next day it was obvious that the gauntlet had been thrown down, and all the lunches were a credit to the wives.

The fifth and last day was "Showdown Time". When we had climbed the stairs to the tower, Jim Franklin announced that he was providing lunch, with the help of the other four. He produced fried chicken on a platter, tossed a Caesar salad (raw egg and all), and served lunch on a tablecloth with napkins, silverware, and candlesticks. I protested that I could not go home without opening the lunch that Hope had provided, and they agreed. She had peeled a large tomato and spread it open, and covered it with crab meat and a Louie dressing. This was accompanied by thin sandwiches of rye bread spread with butter, chopped Basil, and a dusting of Parmesan. My lunch was divided and served to all, and we considered the battle of the lunches to be a draw. Word had spread through the offices of the "lunch battle" in the tower, so we had dozens of visitors.

Two days later I was scheduled for my check ride with
Hugh Gourdin to Honolulu and Los Angeles. I parked my
car briefly in front of the crew check-in door, while I carried
in my Halliburton suitcase and briefcase. As I reached the
door Jim Franklin was just coming out. He held the door
open for me, and as I walked past him he asked; "Tom, which
bag has your lunch?".

Flights across the extreme northern latitudes of America
have a unique problem. The magnetic North Pole is
somewhere north of Hudson Bay, about a thousand miles
from the true North Pole, so in that part of the world the
compass is practically worthless. In 1956 the Sperry
Instrument Company developed the "Polar Path Compass"
for use in the DC-7C aircraft. This was actually a directional
gyro with controllable precession, but the airline turned it
into a catch phrase for advertising. The advertisements
claimed we were flying the Polar Route to London, when
we were never within a thousand miles of the North Pole.
But from the west coast we were on a much shorter path to
Europe, the so-called Great Circle route, with a greatly
reduced travel time from the traditional route through New
York. A fueling and crew change stop was needed, so
Frobisher Bay, on Baffin Island in the Northwest Territories
of Canada, was selected.

The company bought a pre-fabricated hotel and had it
barged into Frobisher, just ahead of winter. It was large
enough to accommodate two crews, plus the ground staff of
mechanics, cooks, dispatchers, and other personnel. Winter
temperatures were usually around -40 degrees, and the wind
blew constantly, so outdoor activities were minimal In winter.
On leaving San Francisco the Engineers were issued
sheepskin winter gear and boots so that we could preflight
the airplane in Frobisher and make repairs. A heavy rope
was strung on posts for a distance of a quarter mile between
the hotel and the dispatch office so we wouldn't get lost in
the blowing snow.

Winter in the far north is not friendly to the ill prepared, so we each received a one-day ground-school course in winter survival techniques. Fred Tubbs was the instructor and did an excellent job of it. One of the Engineers was so impressed by what he learned that he named the class "Terror on the Tundra". The Chief Pilot thought it would be a good idea if the crewmembers learned how to build an igloo during the layovers, and a local Eskimo was hired to conduct classes in their construction. After you and your team had built the igloo you were given a candle, sleeping bag, and the privilege of spending the night in snowbound comfort.

Through the long winter the Mounties dropped in occasionally, mainly to check out the stewardesses. They and the few locals regaled us with stories about the Arctic Char fishing in summer. The Char is similar to a steelhead trout, and is reputed to be one of the fiercest fighting fish in the world and I could hardly wait. Come July the ice went out of the river, and the fish came in. The company had bought some fishing tackle for our use, but the lures quickly wound up snagged on rocks in the bottom of the river. In London, I asked the hall porter at the Kensington Palace hotel where I might buy some fishing lures, and he helpfully gave me the name of a store on New Bond street called Farlow's. I walked up and down that short street several times before finding the store. It did not look like what I expected in the way of sporting goods, as there was nothing in the front window but a few antique pictures of fly fishermen. But the name was on the door, so I walked into a wood-paneled room with just a few tables and chairs, and more pictures on the wall. As the door closed a little bell rang in the back room, and an elderly gentleman in a swallow-tailed coat came out to greet me. I thought I must be in the wrong place, so when he asked if he could help me, I said that I was looking for some fishing lures, but must be in the wrong store. He said; "What will you be fishing for, and where?" I gave him the quick answer that I would be hunting the Arctic Char in

Frobisher Bay, Northwest Territories, Canada. Without batting an eye he pulled a drawer of lures out of the wall, put it on a table and said; "You will want the Mepps #5, sir." I bought an assorted dozen #5 lures for about fifty cents each.

The next day at Frobisher, along with the other members of the crew, I walked the half-mile to the river. I made a short cast of about ten yards to study the action of the new lure, and was startled to see four or five large fish chasing it. Suddenly I had a fish on and was hanging on for dear life. The fish and I raced up and down that rocky riverbank for fifteen minutes before he finally came ashore. I caught a six or seven-pound fish on each of my first four casts. I was soon besieged by the rest of my crew for the use of one of those lures. Needless to say, I came to know Abner at Farlow's quite well, and bought many more Mepps lures from him.

I staggered back to the quarters with 25 lbs of Arctic Char, cleaned them, and put them in the walk-in freezer until departure time the next day. I did not want to let the fish defrost during the long flight home so I securely tied the package to the structure inside the nose wheel well, fully removed from the operating machinery and cabin heat. On arrival in San Francisco, with Customs and Immigration officials watching, I climbed up on the nose wheel, untied the frozen package, and carried it into the Customs area. The next week the Chief Pilot put out a bulletin to all crewmembers prohibiting the carriage of any personal luggage in the nose wheel well. Don Kinkle, the Chief Pilot, had added a note to my copy that said, "Tom, what kind of lure were you using?"

MORE STEWARDESSES

By the mid-1950s the oriental passengers were becoming an important part of Pan American's market in the Pacific. Tokyo and Hong Kong were huge sources of revenue, and the company searched for ways to attract more business travelers and tourists from Asia.

In 1955 the decision was made to hire cabin attendants proficient in the oriental languages. Notices were placed in newspapers in Hawaii and the west coast of the U.S. that Flight Attendant jobs were available to those with suitable language skills. A training school was initiated in Honolulu and soon the first of several hundred girls started training. In a few weeks we saw a trickle of charming oriental girls on our Stratocruiser crews. They were all based in Honolulu and flew from there to San Francisco, Los Angeles, Tokyo and Hong Kong. It was a great success with the Asian passengers, and with the American passengers as well.

Very soon a few problems cropped up. On several occasions one of the Nisei girls came to the cockpit in tears, and had to sit in the "Jump seat" for a few minutes to compose herself before returning to the cabin. One explained to me that some of the Japanese passengers treated her very rudely, as if she were a low servant. Most of these girls had college degrees and were not accustomed to that kind of treatment. Many of them told me that they did not like to serve Japanese passengers. One theory held that

125

many Japanese passengers knew that some of these Nisei girls were descendants of the Japanese who left Japan to work in the plantations of Hawaii. Therefore they were assumed to be of a lower class.

In a year or so these girls became senior enough to transfer to other crew bases. They wanted to see Europe, Africa, and Latin America, as well as the Orient. Fortunately the Asian people were traveling all over the world in increasing numbers, so those language skills were put to good use on all of the airline's routes. Those lovely oriental girls added a unique charm to the cabin service all over the world.

From the very beginning one of the hiring requirements for cabin attendants was the ability to speak a foreign language. Not well, mind you, but passably able to communicate. As the European economies improved, more and more of our passengers did not speak English. Advertisements were placed in major newspapers all over Europe, seeking applicants for Flight Attendant jobs. Many of those hired were proficient in several languages. They were sent to a new training school in Miami, where during their training, they were given a form to fill out listing their home base preferences. Choices offered were New York, Miami, Los Angeles, San Francisco, or Seattle. Whichever they chose, the assignment was usually New York, the least desirable base for most. And again, within a year they were exercising their seniority and moving to another base. The Scandinavians wanted to go to Hawaii, or Los Angeles. The French and Italians wanted San Francisco. In the end it all worked out very well, and all the bases had a wonderful diverse group of cabin attendants. I often listened in on the public address system with pride while the Purser introduced the cabin attendants, and each said a few words in her native language.

At the same time the airline was hiring pilots and engineers in large numbers, many of them young and single.

Predictably, with so many wonderful girls, the new hired pilots were like blind dogs in a butcher shop!

The airline found great success in glamorizing the cabin with female attendants. As a result very few males were hired at that time, but some of the few were exceptional. I remember a charming Frenchman named Jean Ptak. While having lunch with him in Bangkok I told him of the disaster my wife and I encountered while trying to make a Hollandaise sauce. It would not stay creamy, but insisted on separating into a granular mess. He said that the secret was to stir it with a wooden spoon in a copper bowl, using a figure eight motion. We tried it, but that did not work either. (The real secret is to add a tablespoon of warm water.)

At that time all the Pan American crew members stayed at the same hotel, so we frequently dined together. The three or four old gray-haired veterans often escorted five or six young, attractive ladies to dinner (dutch, of course) to the puzzlement of the other diners. If we were feeling gallant, dinner might be followed by dancing at the Royal Hawaiian Hotel, or a walk on the beach at Waikiki. Those are still good memories.

When we knew that there was a brand new girl in the crew on our flight to Honolulu it was fun to celebrate her first trip with a classic evening on Waikiki. A Mai-Tai at the beachside bar at the "Outrigger Canoe Club", followed by a mahi-mahi dinner in the club dining room. We might stop at one of the tourist places to hear someone sing "Tiny Bubbles", or look in on the Don Ho show, but it was always a night to remember, for all of us.

JETS

Of course we knew they were coming, and that the airline business would go through some big changes. But how it would affect us individually made us all a bit nervous. Obviously there would be another cycle of increased productivity with the faster speed and higher capacity of the jets, and the inevitable furloughs of junior cockpit personnel. For the Flight Engineers there were several new things to worry about.

These new aircraft were going to be very different from the piston machines. The jet engines are very simple, with few moving parts subject to wear, and no controls other than the Power Lever, or throttle. But now we were going to have some very sophisticated electrical equipment. No more 24-volt direct current generator systems, now it would be 115-volt alternating current equipment at 400 cycles frequency. And the four engine-driven alternators would be linked electrically together (paralleled) to create one very large electrical source. By 1956 the word had trickled down that we had better start thinking electronically, because that was the way it was going to be. I wanted to be ready, so I searched about in bookstores and libraries, but at that time there was very little there to help me. I enrolled in a correspondence course in radio and television repair from DeVry Technical Institute. This was the only thing I could find that would bear on my future studies of the Boeing 707 aircraft, and it might give me a bailout occupation in the future. The course was excellent. I built an oscilloscope, a vacuum tube voltmeter, other test equipment, and I managed to get a good grip on electronics. In addition, with recognition of the new developments in transistors, there was a course in their study. I learned that the Westinghouse Company was designing and building the electrical system for the 707 aircraft, so I wrote a letter to them requesting information on the equipment. Their reply was that for $5.00 they would send me the Red Book, which described the whole system. I bought the book and spent months reading the 250 pages. I read it four times, and almost memorized it. When my turn came to start ground school on the 707, I certainly had a leg up because I was well prepared on the electrical system. Indeed I was knowledgeable enough that the Chief Flight Engineer asked if I would be willing to avail myself to the maintenance department for troubleshooting help on the 707 electrical systems.

Without a doubt the development of the Jet engine was the most spectacular advance in the history of air transportation. The Pratt & Whitney JT4 engine, as used in the 707 aircraft, moved airline travel into an unbelievable level of public acceptance. A trip of a few thousand miles became a casual inconvenience for most, and the "white knuckles" virtually disappeared. In a few short years the public attitude on air travel changed completely from excitement to boredom. Soon we were looking at in-flight movies, stewardesses in short skirts, and eating packaged meals. The whole feeling of international travel changed quickly. With over a hundred people jammed into a 707 the crews began to refer to them as "Cattle Cars", and some of the glamour disappeared. We found ourselves carrying our briefcases through endless terminal walkways, and sometimes our suitcases as well. It was expedient, but the old Pan Am image had faded a bit. If anything, that image was now one of some "Old Pros" with gray hair and an expanding waistline, and some "senior" stewardesses wearing "support hose".

Nevertheless the jets were a pleasure, and a tremendous improvement for the crews. In addition to the delights of a higher salary (we called it Kerosene Pay), there was the lower noise level, the lack of vibration, the greatly increased reliability, and the prestige. Those JT4 engines would run forever, and it was a thrill to be harnessed to four of them. Now we had a quiet confidence on take-off that everything would function well, and I found that I slept better. As reliability soared, so did on-time performance. Of course, there were a few glitches along the way. One was a minor problem with the pneumatic system. An air pipe ran through the wing leading edges to each engine. Its purpose was to supply high-pressure bleed air from the engines, or a ground "Start Cart", to operate the pneumatic starters, as well as the air conditioning systems. At each engine there was a check valve to isolate that engine from the manifold pipe if it was not running. If that valve did not close properly it would leak so much air overboard that the engine starters would not work.

On one occasion, by dawn's early light in the Fiji Islands, the check valve on # 2 engine hung open. I called downstairs for the passenger ramp to be brought to the forward door, went down and opened the right side cowling on number 2 engine. While a ramp worker held the cowling open, I took the 4 by 4 timber used as a wheel block on the nose tire, and gave the offending valve a good rap. It obediently closed with an audible snap, and while he closed the cowling I climbed the stairs back to the cockpit. Halfway up the stairs I saw a first-class passenger, bug-eyed, watching me through the window. In the modern world of high technology, it is hard to accept the occasional use of a 4 by 4 piece of timber.

The Airline Pilots Association (ALPA) is the big dog in the airline labor arena. It has tremendous power over the airlines, and knows how to use its muscle to get what all the pilots want. Now there was the prospect that many junior pilots were going to be furloughed as the jets were phased in. Fewer crews were needed, and cutbacks were inevitable. ALPA headquarters in Chicago focused on the third seat in the cockpit—mine. If I could be eliminated, a junior pilot could fill my job and fewer ALPA members would lose their jobs. The airlines were not very happy with the prospect of training thousands of pilots to become licensed Flight Engineers, and my group was not willing to be displaced, so the conflict was established. Most of the senior pilots wanted to keep the professional engineers, rather than have a newly trained pilot sitting in the third seat, but ALPA was running the show. My union, the Flight Engineers International Association (FEIA) was a rather puny affair compared to the mighty ALPA. As the pilots increased pressure on the airlines it became obvious that we were going to lose our cause and our jobs. With no one to turn to we decided that our only hope for survival was the drastic action of a strike. On the chosen day, every Flight Engineer in the country walked off and we shut down all the major airlines in the United States for seven days. That brought the desired attention. President Kennedy intervened, appointing a neutral Commission to resolve the issue. The engineer's union quickly agreed to accept the Commission's decision, as did the airlines. The pilot's union found themselves between a rock and a hard place. If they agreed, the junior pilots might lose their jobs. If they did not agree they would become the bad guys, so they went along. We picketed for just one day. Jim Chadwick and I were assigned to picket in front of the downtown ticket office on Union Square in San Francisco. The two of us spent the whole day in uniform, walking up and down the street and carrying a picket sign. One old gentleman, probably retired Navy, was very upset and chewed me out for picketing while "wearing that uniform". I explained that it was an airline uniform, but he was still mad. The sales staff in the

Stockton Street office supported our cause, and kept us supplied with coffee, soup, and sympathy. The next day, when the airlines did not try to mount any kind of a scheduled operation, further picketing was cancelled. I was on vacation that month and, it being Easter week with the boys out of school, Hope and I had rented a cabin at Squaw Valley for a week of skiing. For the rest of the week I nervously listened to the morning radio news, and then tried to enjoy a day on the slopes with my family.

Professor Nathan P. Feinsinger was a well-respected government arbitrator, with the reputation of being very thorough in his investigations into the merits of every case. We were pleased that he was appointed to study our cause because we felt that he would be fair. He was thorough. His staff sat in on simulator sessions, training flights, and rode in the jump seat on scheduled flights. We found his ultimate decision a full vindication of our complaint. Ultimately he ruled that the job was ours, but we would have to obtain pilot qualifications, at company expense. And the airline must carry a third pilot on the 707s until we had achieved those qualifications. For those who chose not to accept the terms there was the option of a $40,000 severance pay and about 20 men took it. Dr Feinsinger further said that the airlines could offer pilot positions to Engineers who qualified, but that never happened.

The extra pilot sat in a jump seat behind the Captain and, on very rare occasions, might be granted a take-off or landing. To maintain qualification a commercial pilot must have made three take-offs and landings within the previous ninety days. These extra pilots rarely met that requirement, so every three months would be scheduled for a training flight. Sometimes there were five or six of them on the training flight, and each would do the needed two or three take-offs and landings, and go back into the cabin to eat his box lunch and read a magazine until the final landing. One of the third pilots told me that from his jump-seat perch he spent most of his time studying the Captains haircut.

Over 600 Pan American Flight Engineers obtained a Commercial Pilot license with Instrument Rating. There were no incidents and no injuries. Most of us already had a very old private pilot's license, but chose not to mention it in order to take advantage of the full course. Flight Safety International administered my training at San Carlos airport, south of San Francisco. During training I learned that the flying school was due to receive two new Cessna aircraft, so I asked how the airplanes would be delivered, suggesting that I could fly one from the Wichita factory on a long cross-country flight. The school was delighted with the idea, especially when I confessed that I had a private pilot's license. John Aikens had just earned his private pilot's license, and he volunteered to go with me and fly the second airplane to San Carlos as part of his training. The school paid for our discount ticket on UAL, and our expenses (and charged Pan American for every hour we flew). I took my son Jack along, but young Curt Aikens had to cancel at the last minute because of a bad cold. We enjoyed a tour of the Cessna factory, and then flew the southern route to California. East of Albuquerque we were doing about 85 mph but bucking a 25 mph headwind when John called me on the radio to report that all the cars on the interstate highway below were passing us. In addition to a steady stream of Flight Engineer students, the school had a large number of young men hoping to catch the wave of airline hiring. Very few pilots were coming out of the military, and the airlines were buying 707 aircraft as fast as Boeing could build them. In four or five months a raw beginner could earn the Commercial Pilot license and Instrument Rating, and the next week become an airline pilot.

I enjoyed the training. Because of my long legs, the usual Cessna 150 aircraft was a bit cramped for training maneuvers, so I did most of my flying in the larger, four-place, Cessna 172. That made it possible to take my three sons along on some of the required cross-country flights. When I returned to line flying I was eager to improve my knowledge of en-route airways procedures, so I studied some of the airways charts. Most of the heavily-traveled air corridors entail very complex routes. A few months after completing training I was on a flight to Orly airport in Paris from Heathrow in London, and had studied the preliminary routing and airways clearance. On departure climb-out I realized the co-pilot had selected the wrong radial on the VOR receiver. He was busy on the radio so I tapped the Captain on the shoulder and pointed to my chart. He laughed and said;

"Hey Tom, you have the charts and everything. Do you know how to read them?"

I said; "Well enough to know you are on the wrong radial".

I pointed to the correct radial on the co-pilot's chart. As he made the correction London Control called and asked what our intentions were. The co-pilot told them that we were correcting on course. I am sure that the training made us all better Flight Engineers. After completing the Commercial Pilot and Instrument licenses we were sent to Miami for a two-hour training session flying a DC-4 aircraft, and then a two-hour session on the 707.

Some of the engineers were upset that we did not have the option of moving to a front-window seat but I think most of us were content to stay with the nuts and bolts part of flying. We only had to maintain a Second Class medical license, and the prospect of working our way back up a seniority list was daunting. The junior pilot in the system would usually wind up in Miami as co-pilot on the medium range Boeing 727, or possibly in Berlin. And advancement would require a family move almost every year between New York, Miami, San Francisco, Seattle, or Berlin. I knew my job well and I felt respected. And the last thing we wanted was to move from our home in Mill Valley. If the airline had offered me a pilot assignment I would have turned it down.

Seniority is the name of the game. The top dog gets whatever he wants, and the rest fight over the scraps. Equipment assignments, vacations, and individual monthly flying assignments all depend on your number on the seniority list. When the last B377 Stratocruisers were retired, everything was flown on the 707s, so the variety on our monthly bid lines was astounding. I could bid for trips around the world, anywhere in the Pacific, London, Paris, Rome, Alaska. If I wanted to avoid the jet lag I could fly to Caracas, or Panama, and back. Or just shuttle to Hawaii and home. Some of the crewmembers spent days going over the monthly bid-lines to figure what they wanted to try for in the next lottery. There were so many things to consider; golf dates, little league games, boy scout outings, even the wife's menstrual cycle. If they were in the nether regions of the seniority list, their bid was a shot in the dark, but still worth a try. The senior men might mail in a bid card with only three or four choices picked, while the junior man filled the card with choices. As my seniority improved I elected the sunshine approach. During our winter months I bid for trips to Australia, New Zealand, and Tahiti. Summer it was London, Tokyo, and Hong Kong. And I always felt sorry for those guys who were working for a domestic airline and flying shuttles to Los Angeles or Seattle, or Miami. Or Fresno.

The late 1960s truly were the glory days for Pan American. Airline routes and fares were still regulated, kerosene was 10 cents a gallon, and the competition was still staying behind us. PanAm's stock price soared to new highs. The Boeing Company was working as fast as it could, but it was hard to keep up with the demand for new aircraft. Soon every man who had been furloughed was called back to work, and middle-aged co-pilots were finally getting their captain's stripes. The military pilots started to leave the service in droves and apply at five or six airlines, then faced the problem of which one to choose when they all offered employment. Most of them wanted to go to PAA, and they all expected to be captains within two years. Right. The profits rolled in for the airlines and the company set off on some grand expansion plans with a hotel division, aerospace subcontracting, and the biggest office building in New York City. The unions wanted a piece of it too, and the new working agreements featured large pay raises and greatly sweetened pensions. Medical retirement benefits were instituted, providing half pay until retirement age, when the beneficiary received normal retirement pay. We had never had it so good. The company built huge training centers in New York, San Francisco, and Miami, and the new flight simulators were busy around the clock.

Pan American eventually gave up on professional Flight Engineers as the numbers were just too great to cope with. Thousands of pilots were available, but few mechanics wanted to become Engineers. Of course ALPA was still pushing for an all ALPA cockpit, and suddenly we were Dodos. Dead Dodos, but with grandfather rights. Training was moved up to a frantic pace to try to keep up with aircraft deliveries and expanding schedules. Again I was recruited to be an Instructor and Check Airman. The job paid a higher salary, but also had some fringe benefits. I found the training work interesting because the airline had been very careful to hire the best of the applicants, and they were a sterling group. Now instead of being the young kid teaching the old pros I was the old pro teaching some very sharp young pilots, and sometimes I had to struggle to stay ahead of them. The greatest benefit of teaching lies in what you learn in the process, and my students had a great deal to contribute from their military background. The former military men made good Engineers because they gave the job everything they could, while many of the civilian trained pilots were bored with the whole thing and just wanted to move on towards that left seat.

Charles Lindbergh served for years on the Pan American Board of Directors, and as he was one of Juan Trippe's most trusted advisors, he was very involved in decisions on new equipment and routes. As a member of the board he was entitled to a seat in first-class but he never took it, preferring to travel quietly under an assumed name. He kept a very low profile, and was always seated in the rear section of the cabin on the left side, about five rows forward of the rear entry door. He preferred a window seat, and he always wore a hat. I made it a practice to walk the length of the cabin on every flight to look and listen for problems, such as leaking entry door seals, sagging ceiling panels, rumbling bearings on recirculation fans, or water leaks in the galley areas. And a quick peek out each wing at the aileron positions to confirm trim control settings. And it felt good on a long trip to stretch my legs. Several times I spotted Lindbergh, and, upon invitation, he would always follow me back to the cockpit for a half hour chat about what the airline was doing. I am not claiming that I knew him, but he recognized me, and called me "Tom". On one occasion I had a student Flight Engineer with me. I introduced everyone in the cockpit, and Lindbergh talked about some of the new navigation aids that interested the company. Then he excused himself to resume his nap. After he left, the former Air Force Colonel who was my student asked me who that guy was. When I told him he said, "Gawd, I thought he was dead!"

Eventually the company bought 130 Boeing 707 aircraft, 19 Douglas DC8s, and scads of Boeing 727 and 737 airplanes. And the training department had a hard time keeping up. Let me make a point. I served for 12 years on the 707, and 12 years on the 747. In 24 years I spent a total of 10 weeks in ground school, aside from brief required recurrent training classes. A typical new hire had two to three months of initial training to qualify on his first aircraft, say a 727, and pass the Flight Engineer license requirements. Within a year he would bid for a higher paying job as engineer on the 707, and go back into training for eight to ten weeks. A year later he gets a vacancy as copilot on the 727, and is back in ground school. Next is a slot as engineer on the Jumbo, and so it goes. Some of those pilots spent 20 percent of their career in training, while I spent less than 2 percent of my time there. And training is a very big expense. In addition to paying a salary to a non-productive pilot, the instructors and facilities are very expensive; training flights cost thousands of dollars an hour, and in many cases the student must be housed and fed. Then he and his family, and his furniture and automobiles must be moved. The airline would have saved a bundle if they had stayed with professional engineers. But I must admit that the years spent in the middle seat helped to produce pilots with a better knowledge of their aircraft and its operation.

During these years the company began to find some stiff competition from every corner of the globe. Every country wanted a national airline, and they were encouraged by American policies of federally backed low interest loans on the purchase of new American-made aircraft. American flag carriers had to pay the going rate for financing purchases, but any banana republic could buy a 707 for a small down payment and low interest, and open an airline. They frequently offered travel packages well below the normal rates to encourage tourism. The North Atlantic became a maze of dozens of airlines flying the same routes, shoulder to shoulder, and a new gimmick developed. If you wanted to go to Rome, Alitalia had some great deals for you. To Greece, Olympic could provide the best price, with hotels, tours and air-fare packages well below what the American flag carriers could offer. Tourism became a subsidized national industry, and PanAm could not compete. Soon the North Atlantic routes became a necessary but money-losing operation. Across the Pacific, Tokyo became the hub, and Japan Air Lines had firm control of Japan. Any attempt by PanAm to increase frequency was doomed to three or four years of negotiations, and was only allowed in return for greatly increased access to the American market by JAL. Gradually PanAm's turf was being nibbled away by other airlines and government agencies, and all efforts to obtain some domestic ties to our International routes were doomed to start with. Pan American Airways had pioneered service to Juneau, Alaska in the mid 1930s, even built the first airport there, but in the mid sixties the politicians decided that another airline should have exclusive rights to that route. I was walking down the hall to the dispatch office in Tokyo when I stopped to look at the daily company news wire. It usually had things like delay reports, load factors, and other dull information, but that day was different. It said;

> *"There's a land where the mountains are nameless,*
> *and the rivers all run God knows where.*
> *There are lives that are erring and aimless,*
> *And deaths that just hang by a hair.*
>
> *There are hardships that nobody reckons,*
> *There are valleys unpeopled and still.*
> *There's a land, Oh, it beckons and beckons,*
> *And I want to go back, and I will.*
>
> ("The Spell of the Yukon", Robert Service)

And the message was signed; "Pan Am Juneau, 1935-1965, shutting down." I stood in front of the message and almost wept, then carefully copied it on the back of an envelope.

Soon almost every domestic carrier had international routes, and PanAm had brutal competition. TWA had always, since the war. served half of the European area, Continental started a daily non-stop from Dallas to Honolulu, Braniff did so too and invaded Central and South America, and each of them could draw passengers from their network of domestic

routes. PanAm losses mounted, and there seemed to be no
way to stop them. It was difficult to sell a ticket to London to
a person in Chicago, because United could provide better
connections. TWA had almost the entire United States
interior to feed their flights to Europe, and United soon
"owned" the service to Hawaii with their tremendous
domestic connections.

JUMBO

Two headlights were down there at the end of the tunnel; The SST, and the 747.

Always the leader, in this case reluctantly, Pan American Airways ordered some Anglo-French SST airliners, the Concordes, and hoped that the American manufacturers would build one as well. The European track record had not been very good on new designs, and the tragedy of the early de Havilland Comet was still there.

During a golf game in Seattle, Juan Trippe persuaded Bill Allen, President of Boeing, to build the Boeing 747 for PanAm. They were old friends. Many years earlier, Trippe had convinced Allen that Boeing should build the 707, and both companies had profited well from that venture. At that time a strong impetus to the Boeing and Douglas companies came from the PanAm Chief Engineer, Andre Priester. When de Havilland announced the construction of the first Jet transport airplane, Andre Priester sent a wire to Bill Allen and Donald Douglas. It simply said;

"The British are coming!"

The Concorde couldn't pass muster. There was just no way that anyone could make it pay its way, unless you had the advantage of the British or French treasury. But a 400-passenger Boeing 747 airplane made a lot of sense, and was very exciting to the employees. Obviously the pay would be good, plus the thrill of flying the biggest airplane in the world. And we were going to be first!

In 1967 I returned to line flying, again. I found that I became too critical after a couple of years of being a Check Airman. It was very difficult when I was faced with the prospect of turning down someone whom I knew well, perhaps a friend of 25 years. When I had trouble sleeping I knew it was time to quit the office and return to line flying.

In 1965 we had purchased Kiski Lodge, a hotel on Donner Summit adjacent to the Sugar Bowl ski resort. My sons, by this time aged 14, 12, and 10 had all become excellent skiers, but it was an expensive sport. We rationalized that buying the hotel would be an appropriate investment for our family, and would provide some tax relief while paying for our recreation. It worked out well, but it did require a great deal of time. We had a full time staff of five, who could handle the weekday customers, but my family had to be there at the weekends to help with the 50 or 60 customers. The boys learned many skills, from cooking to plumbing, and skied for free. My seniority had improved to the point that I could almost design my schedule, so that I was able to be home almost every weekend for the Friday night trek to the mountains and the Sunday night return. The first and second year were a bit rocky, but we finally found our niche with youth groups, and it went well after that. After five years the end came when I was in Roswell, New Mexico for a month on a training assignment. The boys were involved in school activities, and my wife was the only one available to make the weekend trip to the hills. Shortly after that weekend we sold the hotel, at a good profit, fortunately.

In the summer of 1969 Pan American expected the first 747 aircraft to arrive in October. Chief Flight Engineer John Shively called and suggested that I should come back for another assignment in the office. I hesitated until he offered me a spot in the first training class for the new airplane, and a Check job on it. I went back to the office the next day.

After being one of the last on the flying boats I was going to be one of the first on the Jumbo Jets. On September 1,1969, 14 Flight Engineers, plus one FAA Inspector, started ground school on the 747. Our instructors had only a limited knowledge about the airplane, and had to call Boeing several times a day to be able to answer questions raised in class. One of them had the habit, when asked a difficult question, of gazing at the ceiling, and then saying "Yes", "No", "Maybe", or, "I'll call Boeing". During a coffee break Jocko Parrish and I marked some papers with those responses in large letters, taped them to the classroom ceiling, and waited. It was a classic double take, and broke up the class. As we neared the end of our five-week class the airline announced that the aircraft delivery dates were delayed for several months. Rather than just send us home to wait, the company decided to break us up into small teams and have us draw up some training aids for future classes. I spent two months researching the very complicated hydraulic systems, drawing schematic diagrams, and tape recording some talking books, which were copied and sent to the New York and Miami training bases. The rest of the class were doing similar things on Powerplants, Electrical Systems, Landing Gear, Controls, and other areas, so we all shared the information we had found. It turned into an excellent training exercise. As yet, we did not have a full Simulator, but we had a plywood and cardboard mockup that Bob Stubbs made and it served for procedure drills. The call came at the end of the year and we were ready.

ROSWELL

The 747 was not yet a certificated airplane, but Boeing loaned two of them to Pan American to start the training program in Roswell, New Mexico. On January 2, 1970, about 40 of us boarded an airplane we had never seen before and went to Roswell, where we found 6 inches of snow on the ground. Roswell was a town that had almost died. The huge Walker Air Force Base had been the core of its economy for many years, and the B-36 bombers trailing around the traffic pattern on their training missions were part of a normal day. When the military left it became very quiet. One developer had the bad fortune to be on the verge of finishing a 36-unit subdivision of large homes when the announcement came. The bank foreclosed and was offering them at bargain prices, so one of our pilots bought one and moved to Roswell. The city inherited the air base, and the job of maintaining and trying to support it. They had not been very successful, at that time, in finding any rent-paying industry, so they were very pleased when Pan Am started to use the base as a training facility. For several years we had been doing the 707 training there, and it proved to be an ideal spot for the early surge of training on the Jumbo. There was an Instrument Landing installation, a control tower, and nobody else in the air. Hotels were cheap and available, and the weather was usually good, in that the wind blew and provided a challenging environment to the transitioning pilots. We could do a lot of training in a very short time because we had the place almost to ourselves. On my first training flight we went through all the required procedures in two hours, and I was signed off as qualified. The next day I took two students on their first training flight, and my second. They were the senior engineers from American Airlines, preparing to operate one of Pan Ams first 747s on a lease basis. I spent the month of January in cold, windy Roswell, and did not see a single UFO, or much else since there isn't a great deal to see. The prospect of a month sitting in a motel room between training flights was not very pleasing so I went looking for a rental car. The front desk at the motel said that there were no rental car agencies in Roswell, so I walked downtown to the Auto Row, where one dealer had a nice line up of about 20 used cars for sale. I liked the look of a blue 1962 Cadillac Coup de Ville. The owner of the business, Billie Durham, was eager to make a sale but I had a better deal for him. I said I would test drive the car for three weeks, and every Monday would check in with him, and give him $25 in cash. After a few minutes the message sank in and he agreed. The car did not run very well but Fitch Robertson and I dug out our tool kits and tuned it to perfection. For six months my succeeding instructors stopped by every Monday to drop $25 on a delighted Billy Durham.

The training was sporadic because the new airplane had a few major problems and was frequently down for maintenance. A second airplane arrived but it too had the same problems. The biggest headache was the complicated wing flap system. All those levers and pivots inside the 'canoe," or plastic wing flap drive cover would get out of synchronization and something would break. It always happened with the flaps partially extended so the airplane had to limp back to the huge hangar and wait for parts from the Boeing factory. A re-design was quickly done, but it put a crimp in our training program. The second big problem was the mounting of the engine. Hung from the top it did not adequately support the sides of the engine. This allowed the round engine case to distort into a slight oval, which created compressor spillage and caused the engine to backfire violently, or stall. It took a long time to design and instal a yoke type engine mount to correct the problem, so we coped with a temperamental engine for several years. Then there was the problem of the evacuation slides. When one of the main cabin's ten doors was closed the slide was "armed" for automatic deployment as soon as anyone started to open the door from the inside, unless another lever was moved to deactivate the system. Captain Don Kinkle, Vice President of Operations, came out from New York to look in on the program and went on a training flight. After they taxied into the ramp at the end of the session he helpfully opened the R-1 (right forward) door and the slide automatically activated. Somebody telephoned the news to the motel and we were all waiting to razz him when he got off the bus. Don took it well. He said it was the biggest erection he had ever seen.

Roswell had lots of very authentic Mexican eating places, and a few fancy restaurants, but we soon found the most reasonable and reliable place was Luby's cafeteria. The students showed up for a few days of training, were checked out and went home to wait for the certification of the aircraft and the start of scheduled operations. In the evening there might be twenty or more crew-members at Luby's, and our Coup de Ville was always full when we left the motel for dinner.

The high point of my stay at Roswell was the Demonstration of Emergency Evacuation required by the FAA for certification of any new aircraft. It had to be demonstrated that a full load of passengers and crew could evacuate the airplane safely in ninety seconds in an emergency. A further restriction was placed on the demonstration: only half of the ten doors could be used, and we did not know which five would be available. Pan Am agreed to run the test at Roswell and everyone got into the act. Two planeloads of FAA people arrived from Oklahoma City, and Boeing, UAL, JAL, and AA sent representatives to observe the test.

A full load of passengers meant 385 people so announcements were put in the local paper, and were made on local radio stations inviting local citizens to participate. On the appointed evening about 600 people showed up for the chance to sit in a giant 747, listen to the music, have a snack, and slide down the evacuation chute. The outside window on each of the exit doors had a red light bulb, covered with aluminum foil, taped over it. Connecting wires ran to a console in front of the nose wheel, where an FAA specialist was ready to flip the switches controlling the red lights. A red light in the door window would indicate to the cabin attendant that that door could not be used for evacuation.

The cockpit crewmembers were newly-qualified airmen from the San Francisco base, as were the dozen cabin attendants. It was mid-January, and very cold with a brisk New Mexico wind, but all the students and instructors lined up at the fence to watch the show. The test was conducted in the early evening to accommodate the working hours of the participants, and to meet a further government demand that it be carried out in darkness. When all doors were closed the floodlights were turned off and we waited in the darkness. We stood in the cold wind for about a half hour watching. Through the passenger windows the cabin attendants could be seen moving in the aisles and giving the emergency instructions, then serving the snack trays.

When all was ready the captain was to order an evacuation over the public address system, and at the same time turn on the red rotating beacon on the bottom of the airplane as a signal that the order was given. Well and good, except that the crew put the beacon switch in the Flight position and, the aircraft being on the ground, the beacon did not come on. Since the specialist at the nose of the airplane didn't see a flashing beacon signal none of the red door lights were turned on. The FAA men were startled to see all ten doors suddenly burst open, all ten slides inflate, and one minute later the airplane was empty of people. The feds called foul, and everyone went home. We all went to Luby's for dinner.

Several days later the slides were repacked and installed and another attempt was made, this time with a New York based crew. We were not allowed to use the same passengers again, so more announcements were made and another 600 or so showed up for the test. Again, all the interested parties were there to observe. The rear entry doors are on the tapering part of the fuselage, and require special slides to accommodate the taper. With the wrong slide installed at the R-5 door, one of the attachments came adrift, the slide collapsed, and one of the evacuees suffered a sprained ankle. So again everyone went home, and we went back to Luby's for a post-mortem.

For the third attempt it was necessary to extend the announcements over the border into Texas to ensure a fresh group of passengers, as Roswell was running out of people. With the usual observers on hand, a fresh crew from Los Angeles pulled it off with three seconds to spare, and it was a grand night at Luby's.

At the end of the month Fitch Robertson and I ferried one of the airplanes to San Francisco for maintenance, and during the two-hour flight we wrote up 71 maintenance discrepancies. A few weeks later the newly licensed aircraft arrived and we were ready to launch service from Los Angeles to Honolulu. I was on the third flight to Honolulu and the public acceptance was amazing. The passengers and crew loved the airplane, and every flight was fully booked. In Honolulu people turned out by the thousands just to watch it leave, and it was almost impossible to book a seat. At first nobody seemed to mind the teething problems we were having with the new aircraft, nor the resulting delays. A few weeks later Flight Engineer Sy Tunis and I were sent to Boeing to take delivery of the sixth airplane for Pan Am. We spent one day on a special tour of the factory, did two acceptance test flights, and signed off on the aircraft. The next day, with a full load of fuel, we flew nonstop to Nassau, in the Bahamas and landed. The Pan American rep handed the Boeing rep a check for the balance on the $25 million purchase price, and with three kilos of mail we flew on to JFK for an overnight. In this way the airplane entered the United States in Pan American ownership as a used aircraft, which made a big difference in its value for sales tax purposes. During the overnight stop in JFK the life vests, rafts, and other company-supplied equipment were installed, and the following morning we took the airplane to Los Angeles and it left that night for Honolulu. During the round trip across the USA we never added fuel, so we were able to gather some important data on consumption for Operations Engineering. The transcontinental flight was unusual because of the interest it aroused among the Air Traffic Controllers. When we reported our position to Kansas City Center and told them we were at 41,000 feet, he immediately called back to ask the type of aircraft, as no other civilian transport of that time could climb that high. When we responded we were a 747, a UAL and a TWA flight wanted to know our position, hoping to see us.

The cabin attendants were thrilled with the new airplane; they said it was like performing for an audience of almost 400 people. A variety of new uniforms added some spice to their performance, and the Operations Department soon ordered modified uniforms for the cockpit crew as well. The old, hot, double-breasted coats were discarded for a much more comfortable single breasted jacket, and a more modern wing insignia was supplied to the pilots. The old engineer's half wing, attached to a radial engine, had been replaced earlier by a full pilots wing, reflecting our added qualifications

. The traveling public loved the airplane. It was a great adventure to fly to London, or Honolulu, on the "Jumbo", and it was soon difficult to sell a seat on a dowdy old 707. A whole new generation of passenger handling facilities had to be built at airports all over the world to handle the mass movements, and the surge in air travel caused almost every airport in the world to be upgraded to handle the vast numbers of travelers. Every runway had to be extended and widened, every passenger terminal expanded, and the continuous remodeling had not ended yet. Entire new industries were created to support expanding air travel.

The new International Terminal at San Francisco is an example. Connections to and from international flights frequently entail waits of several hours. With time to kill, transit passengers can enjoy one of the fine restaurants or visit the aviation museum while they wait.

TEETHING PROBLEMS

When you walk around the Jumbo doing a pre-flight inspection it is normal to hear a clicking sound if a breeze is turning the big turbines. The 56 blades on the eight-foot diameter fan are mounted loosely in what are termed "fir tree" slots, so called because the tapered serrations resemble the outline of a fir tree. The blades are free to move radially a bit, and in so doing are somewhat self-balancing, reducing engine vibration. Movement of the blades is limited by a stiffener at mid span, slightly wider than the blade, and as these stiffeners bump against each other they create the "click" if the engine is turning slowly. If you are watching you might see the Flight Engineer reach into the engine and give the fan blade a slight spin to see if it will click. On one of my early 747 trips I was a bit concerned on the flight between Guam and Manila because No. 3 engine was showing a higher vibration level than had previously been recorded. After arrival, the Chief Mechanic, accompanied by a technical representative from the Pratt and Whitney manufacturer came to the flight deck. After I explained my concern the Tech suggested we go out and look at the engine. One look and he started searching for that old "four-by-four". The fan section is "shingled" he explained, and showed me how the blades had shifted enough to be locked together, thus causing the higher vibrations. Then he aimed the four-by-four at the mid-span stiffener at the bottom of the fan and gave it a whack. The "shingles" unlocked with a crash that sounded like a box of china plates dropped on a sidewalk. We learned to enjoy that cheerful clicking on our walk-around inspections.

The early Pratt & Whitney JT9D engines were very sensitive to throttle movement, and had to be handled carefully. They operated just fine if left alone at a steady state power, but any rough handling of the throttle could lead to large problems. This was particularly true when the pilot retarded the throttle and, before the engine had stabilized, opened the throttle again. That would easily create a mismatch between the airflow through the first stage compressor and the second stage resulting in a stall. The burner section was still getting fuel and burning brightly, but the fire had no place to go. In a very short time, perhaps 20 seconds, the engine could exceed the temperature limit and would have to be shut down. The Engineers monitored throttle movement closely, primed to call out a Stall and turn off the Start Lever. A few minutes later, when things had stabilized, the engine was restarted and went happily on its way. If the maximum exhaust temperature was exceeded it meant a very expensive removal and inspection of that engine at the next landing. The new yoke-type engine mount helped to cure this, but the pilots had to be trained carefully in throttle management. Now this was all of thirty years ago, and that engine and airplane have gone through several metamorphoses since then.

The disadvantage of being the first with a new type of aircraft is that there are many things that do not work quite right, the so-called "teething problems". Water lines in the galleys and lavatories leaked. The entertainment systems overheated and cut in and out. Fuel quantity gauges were not reliable. Pneumatic airflow valves refused to function. The in-flight movie system was a nightmare. Boeing and the sub-contractors worked hard to make improvements, but this took time, especially for the improvements to be applied to the early aircraft.

JUMBO TALES

 M ost trips on the 747 were routine shuffles to interesting parts of the world, but there were some special occasions.

MALAYSIA

One of my favorite trips on the 747 was the one to Singapore, by way of Tokyo and Hong Kong and return, because it offered a lot of flying time in a rather short period, and comfortable layovers. By the late 1970s the old Singapore was gone, The Raffles Hotel has survived in a modernized form, but the evening open-air market is now a parking garage. The main street, Orchard Road, has become a concrete tunnel between high-rise office buildings, all looking alike.

At Hong Kong the passengers were frequently shifted from one 747 to another for the continuation to Singapore, and for convenience those transiting from Tokyo could bypass the Immigration and Customs checks and go directly to the departure gate. VIPs (Very Important People) were often offered early boarding, so I was not surprised to find the upstairs lounge full of Asian passengers when I climbed the stairs to the flight deck. As I finished my pre-flight checks an Asian gentleman poked his head through the open door and asked if he could have a look at the cockpit. He was middle aged, I judged, and dressed casually in khaki pants and a white short sleeved shirt. As we still had an hour to wait until departure time, and Captain Dave Quinn and the co-pilot were still in the Dispatch office, I invited him to sit in the pilot's seat and have a good look. As I explained the instruments and controls he seemed very knowledgeable and interested, so I asked him if he was a pilot. He said he was, but only on small planes and fighter jets, nothing with more than two engines. The pilot's arrival interrupted our conversation and he returned to the upstairs passenger cabin. Shortly after leveling off at cruise altitude, a stewardess from the upstairs lounge came to the cockpit to complain that one of the ovens in the galley was not working, and could I please try to fix it? After checking with the pilots I stepped back to take a look at it, and was immediately joined by my friend in the khaki pants. While I repositioned the oven-connecting plug he held my flashlight for me, and we both smiled when the power lights on the oven came on.

On the crew limo to our hotel the Purser told us that the same passenger had invited the whole crew to come to his palace the next day, and he would put on a polo match for us, and a luncheon. I asked her who the guy was, and she said he was the Rajah of Johore. One of the stewardesses decided that she would rather go shopping, but the rest of us agreed to be in the lobby at 9 a.m. for the trip to Johore.

Promptly at 9 a.m., the twelve of us were escorted to two large military vehicles and set off for Johore. Each van had a military driver and an officer in the front passenger seat, Malaysian flags on fender mounts, and it was full throttle all the way. The Causeway between Singapore and Johore is a notorious bottleneck, but we just sailed right through in a special military lane with sirens blaring and lights flashing.

The Rajah and his wife were waiting to greet us, and he told us regretfully that there would be no polo because of the early morning rains. The wet grass made it unsafe for the riders and the horses, so instead he offered a tour of his private zoo, stables, and auto collection. Among the cars in the large storage building was a 1938 Mercedes Benz SSK convertible given to him by his father when he was a child, but his current car of choice was a Ford pick-up truck. He also offered to set up a tour of the old palace. He showed us portraits of the Sultan, and took us to his trophy room where he kept the polo trophies from all over the world. The Sultan was obviously a very old and frail man, so I asked if the Rajah would succeed him. He said no, his older brother was next in line, and he would continue to be the Rajah. I also twitted him about not flying on the national Malaysian airline, but he just smiled and said that he and his family felt safer on Pan Am.

Then followed a two-hour luncheon that is still hard to believe. There must have been ten courses of delicious Malaysian food, each served by an Attendant kneeling by your side with a tray upheld. Several of the twelve offspring had joined us for lunch, and that was eye opening. The older ones were all graduates of American universities, and actively involved in their fathers many business interests, which included gold, timber, oil, and agriculture. What a dynasty! After lunch we had a tour of the stables and its 256 polo ponies, followed by a look at the eight polo fields and grandstand. Laid out end to end, the polo fields also provided an adequate 3,500 foot grass runway for his fleet of small aircraft and helicopters.

"Tuan" excused himself, saying he had many things to catch up on after a long absence, but left us in the hands of a daughter and son for the tour of the old palace. A detachment of the army had been turned out to guard the place as we arrived because of the treasures it contains. Normally it is locked, and not open to the public, and the old caretaker and his staff were bewildered by all the attention. The two children were well schooled, and gave us a very moving picture of the ancient empire and their ancestors. We toured the gold and silver service vaults adjacent to the kitchen, and each of us had a chance to sit on the throne. I recently learned that this old "Palace Palangi" has been turned into a museum. Speeding back to the hotel l could only shake my head in wonder at what we had seen. The next day I asked the girl who had chosen to go shopping what she had bought. "Nothing".

A few years later we learned that the old Sultan had died, but before his demise had decreed that the younger son should succeed him. Two years later our friend, the Sultan Iskander, was selected by the thirteen governors of the Malaysian States to be President of Malaysia for a five-year term.

PASSENGERS

With a potential load of up to 400 passengers the odds are fair that there will be an oddball among them: someone who drank too much liquor, had too many personal problems, or was smoking something affecting their judgment. The pursers and ground staff did a good job of screening passengers before and during boarding, but inevitably a few problem cases got through. The Captain had some plastic handcuffs in his briefcase if needed, and we had a length of rope available, but usually problems could be solved by gentle persuasion. If we had a multiple crew, two of us would put on our coats and hats and visit the cabin to explain to the unruly passenger what would happen on landing if he continued to be a problem: he would be met by the local police and escorted to an unpleasant place, and it might ruin his vacation. It usually worked very well, but there were exceptions. There seemed to be something about the hat that carried authority, rather like the policeman's helmet of the English Bobby. A no nonsense approach was effective as was the enthusiastic support of adjacent passengers. As a last resort the CO2 (Carbon Dioxide) extinguisher was considered an effective weapon. The noise and chilling effect on the eyeballs of a blast was daunting and, if needed, the cast-metal cylinder carried authority. (They are no longer carried on passenger aircraft)

The lavatories on the Douglas DC-7s were on the forward left side of the aircraft. There was a small square window on the upper outside wall, which I found convenient for viewing the left engines in flight. Oil leaks, loose cowling panels, or vibrating engines, all could be readily seen from that window. I left the sliding window shade open when I left the rest room. On a return visit a few hours later I would usually find that someone had closed the shade. It amused me to consider the thought processes of that shy passenger. Perhaps that was the same person who was carrying off all those little paper-wrapped slivers of soap and emptying the Kleenex box of tissues.

For a tourist, the flight from Europe to California over the Polar Route is one of the most spectacular trips I can think of. For example, with a morning departure from London on a jet aircraft the arrival at San Francisco will be in mid-afternoon because of the change in time zones. In the summer months you will often enjoy sunshine all the way, and fabulous views. The green coastal fjords of Greenland are a sharp contrast to the hundreds of miles of serene snow and ice in the interior. Northeastern Canada is a wilderness of thousands of lakes and never-ending forests with hardly a mark of man. After passing Hudson Bay the view slowly becomes more civilized, with occasional fence lines and faint roads or perhaps a rare smudge of smoke from a farmhouse chimney. The fence lines are oriented to the surveyors North-South and East-West lines, so an observer can almost guess the magnetic heading of the aircraft, especially when your contrails shadow is painting a line across the land. In the extensive wheat belt it is easy to see the Canadian-American border because the fence line follows it for hundreds of miles. The climax of the flight is reached at the Canadian (or American) Rocky Mountains. It is one thing to drive across that part of North America, but it is quite another thing to see it from 41,000'. Then southward past Mount Rainer and the peaks of Oregon to the California sentinels of Mount Shasta and Mount Lassen, followed by the broad expanse of the central California valley. Visitors from the compact and crowded parts of Europe are stunned by the magnificence of that ten-hour vista.

On the Asian and Middle Eastern routes cultural problems were frequent. Some brought their own food, and wanted to heat it on portable butane stoves, others wanted to know the direction to Mecca to properly say their prayers. On one trip we had about a dozen weighty Sumo wrestlers in the First Class cabin going from Tokyo to Honolulu. After breakfast they sat down on the floor in the upstairs lounge of the 747, in turn, while the hairdresser did each one's special hair-do. They made a grand entrance for the photographers on arrival in Hawaii, and provided good publicity for their scheduled performances in Honolulu.

Pan American operated a lot of charter flights for the government to military bases throughout the Pacific area, especially during periods of conflict. We frequently flew an empty airplane the short hop from San Francisco to Travis Air Force base to load up a cabin full of military personnel going to Saigon during the Vietnam conflict. Many of the female cabin attendants preferred those trips because it meant a cabin full of well-behaved and appreciative G.I.s. They acquired a sense of their real worth through giving those passengers a pleasant flight, but I have seen more than one stewardess come to the flight deck in tears, in full knowledge that all those fine young men were being placed in danger of their lives.

The passenger list sometimes included USO groups going to entertain the troops. Because these were chartered flights the rules regarding cockpit access in flight were not as rigid as those applied to scheduled trips. We often invited notables to join us on the flight deck, to sit in the extra "jump seat" for take-off and landing. Bob Hope, Danny Kaye, Bing Crosby, Jonathan Winters, and dozens of others were happy to sit with us for a few hours en-route. Bob Hope always did a stand-up routine for the soldiers in the cabin.

The heartbreaker was the "R and R" flights we operated out of Saigon and Danang. There was a festive feel to the flight leaving Vietnam to take the soldiers to Hong Kong or Bangkok for their week of relief from war. There was a very quiet, grim feel to the flights that returned them to combat. Many of the cabin attendants wrote down addresses and telephone numbers, then called or wrote the families when they returned to San Francisco.

As the war continued we were made aware of an alarming threat. The North Vietnamese had acquired some very powerful ground-to-air missiles. They would have liked nothing more than to shoot down a PanAm 747 with 400 soldiers on board. The military authorities said that we were safe if we stayed above 5,000 feet altitude until within five miles of the airbase. The missiles couldn't reach that height, and the five-mile perimeter was considered secure. It must have been exciting to watch a 747, with gear down and full flaps make a diving approach to the runway at Ton Sun Hut air base in Saigon. I know it was interesting from my end of it.

During the two or three hours we were parked on the ramp at Saigon while waiting for departure time, the crew moved to the comfort of the upstairs lounge of the Jumbo. The auxiliary power unit in the tail of the airplane provided electrical power and operated an air conditioning system that could cool the Sahara. Military pilots had full access to the aircraft parking area, so we had many callers. They wanted to see the flight deck, the girls, talk about jobs, and cool off for a while. Some of them eventually came to work at Pan Am.

I know, from personal observation, that this is a very large plane. It is also a very small world. Dozens of times I have run into old friends and family in all manner of places. On an airplane? Yes, many times. And in an oyster bar in London, a sushi bar in Osaka, a ski slope in Austria. I would like to think that this world is a community of friends and relatives.

Medical emergencies were not frequent, but happened often enough that we had received training in CPR and First Aid to cope with most of them. Between New Delhi and Tehran an elderly American man suffered a massive heart attack and died in his wife's arms. The purser's calls on the Public Address system produced two doctors, neither of whom could do anything for him, so we covered his body with a blanket, and advised Pan American Operations at Tehran by radio of the situation. Ground staff made all the necessary arrangements on arrival, and the purser insisted that, to lessen the blow, the widow should room with her at our layover hotel in Tehran. Several of us joined the two of them for breakfast the next morning and helped her to notify family at home, and make the arrangements for shipment of the remains back to Chicago. The next day she flew with us to London for a stopover, and the following day the purser was able to change her schedule and accompany her home to Chicago. Great people made a great airline.

FLIGHT 845
TO TOKYO

With a late morning departure, I know it will be a long time before I have lunch. Hope and I see the boys off to school, then have a full breakfast and talk about the family schedule for the next few days. After a shower and shave I pack my suitcase and load it and my briefcase into the old VW airport car and head for SFO.

The crewmembers are required to check in at least an hour before departure for briefing, and to allow time to perform their pre-departure chores. I usually try to be there at least an hour earlier, in case of a traffic delay or something like a flat tire. From Mill Valley it is less than an hour's drive to the airport, so for an 11:30 departure I am on the road around 9:30.

Stopping in front of the guard gate, I drop my suitcase on the cart marked Flight 845, and check that I have written the flight number on the cardboard crew tag attached to my bag. Then I put my briefcase on the ground inside the gate, and find a place to park the car.

Time permitting I stop at the maintenance office in the hangar to learn what work has been done on my assigned aircraft, and chat with the foremen for a few minutes. Then up the stairs to the second floor office area, and with a fresh cup of coffee from the cafeteria I check my mail box, scan the bulletin board, and go down the hall to the crew scheduling check-in desk. I sign in and got a copy of the crew list. I will need that to be sure I spell the names correctly when I fill out the "Official Flight Log".

A few doors down the hall is the Dispatch Office, my next stop. One or more of the pilots will probably be there, going over the weather charts with one of the dispatchers. As the flight time to Tokyo is in excess of eight hours the FAA requires that we have a multiple crew. With three pilots and two engineers we will each be able to get some rest during the long flight. As I am going over the Flight Time Analysis and the fuel loading form the rest of the crew arrive.

The other engineer and I walk to the guard gate, pick up our briefcases, and board the crew bus for the short ride to the airplane. We may flip a coin to decide who will do the flight deck preflight inspections and work the departure, and who will do the outside and cabin inspections. After climbing the long stairs to the forward left entry door, then up the circular stairway to the flight deck, we secure our briefcases to the floor and review the maintenance logbook, making notes for the pilot briefing.

Kerosene (Jet A fuel) is the lifeblood of a jet aircraft, and plenty of it! One of our most important tasks is to be sure that the dispatcher has his numbers right, and that the correct amount is in the tanks. Quantity guages are not very reliable, so we try to verify the fuel load by two or three methods: the amount of fuel indicated on arrival plus the fuel added, the calculated fuel on arrival plus that added, and as an added check we frequently take a reading from the dripstick at each of the five tanks. For the flight to Tokyo the fuel load will probably be around 35,000 gallons, weighing 210,000 pounds.

Soon, the rest of the crew climb the stairs to the flight deck, and the three pilots are stowing their briefcases and building their nests. Charts, pencils, sunglasses, gloves, and notepads are organized. Seat position is critical, so there is a lot of electric grinding noise as the pilots' seats go back and forth and up and down. The engineer is recording fluid quantity readings and starting his paperwork.

The upstairs galley attendant has brewed a pot of coffee, and arrives to offer a fresh cup. A maintenance representative comes to the flight deck to collect the logbook, which one of the engineers has signed. Now a ground man checks in by inter-phone from his position by the nose wheel to report that the last baggage containers are being loaded.

At the captains request the engineer starts reading the Pre-Start check-list. This is a challenge-and-response procedure, with every item checked and confirmed. With word from the purser that all doors are closed, and confirmation from the engineers warning light panel, the co-pilot notifies Ground Control that Clipper 845 is ready to push back from the gate. With clearance received, the captain asks the ground man to confirm that all landing gear safety pins are removed, then clears the ground crew to push the airplane back.

As the airplane backs into position on the taxiway the engineer starts reading the engine start checklist, and the ground man advises that the ramp area is clear. With all engines running the ground man pulls his plug, steps out on the captain's side, and gives us a thumbs-up. Under taxi instructions from Ground Control the airplane threads its way several miles to the end of the active runway, as the co-pilot receives the Airways Clearance for the flight to Tokyo from ATC (Air Traffic Control)

Company policy is that there will be no unnecessary conversation on the flight deck below 10,000 foot altitude, so it is very quiet as we receive take-off clearance and taxi into position on Runway 28. With take-off checks completed the operating pilot starts the throttles forward and then calls for take-off power. At a full gross weight of 710,000 lb. (about

350 tons) the airplane starts rolling slowly, but as full power is applied the 200,000 total horsepower can be felt and the airplane quickly picks up speed. The engineer is checking engine temperature, and tweaking the throttle settings. The pilots cross-check their airspeed indications, and the acting co-pilot starts to call out critical airspeeds as we near flying speed.

Once airborne, the pilot establishes the optimum nose-up attitude and calls for landing gear retraction, then as the speed increases, orders the wing flaps retracted. At around 1,500 feet, the take-off power is reduced to climb setting and we turn to our departure magnetic heading, with Tokyo somewhere ahead of us. This being a high-density traffic area we keep a close watch around us until above 10,000 feet and clear of the coastal area.

The off duty pilot and engineer go downstairs to the crew rest seats, and the long ocean crossing has begun.

At the Equator the world is turning at a speed of a little over 1,000 mph, but in the northern latitudes its speed is something less than that. Even at a speed of Mach .84 (84 % of the speed of sound) our 747 is not able to make the clock stand still, but it does slow it down quite a bit. With a time change of seven hours between San Francisco and Tokyo, and a flight time of around ten hours, we wil arrive in Tokyo three hours after leaving San Francisco—after we re-set our watches.

The airplane proceeds westward and the sun moves very slowly overhead and then slightly behind us. As the heavy load of fuel is burned the lower gross weight of the airplane allows us to climb to higher altitude in search of more friendly wind conditions. The prevailing winds across the Pacific Ocean are from the west, giving us a headwind of anything from negligible to 200 knots, so every effort is made to obtain the latest and best data. If there is a major change in conditions, we will receive a Re-analysis message from Tokyo or San Francisco Dispatch.

Cockpit routine is purely and simply just watching. The two autopilots are flying the airplane, following orders from one of the three Inertial Navigation computers. The pilots are crosschecking their instruments, monitoring navigation readings, and keeping a watchful eye on the sky ahead. The engineer is trimming throttle settings to maintain the exact cruise speed, doing fuel computations, recording engine readings, and watching for any unwelcome changes. There is also time for some discussion about where to go for dinner in Tokyo, the latest from the rumor mill, and vacation plans—All vital stuff.

Narita airport, about 30 miles east of Tokyo, was built in the middle of a farming area so the descent and landing is flown over a lush green countryside entirely free of tall buildings and other obstacles. After landing, and the completion of arrival procedures it is a short drive to our hotel in the gathering darkness. The hotel has a special dining room for the many airline crew-members, catering to the unusual hours we sometimes keep. It is a great socializing spot where we can talk with some of the New York-based crews as well as with those from other airlines.

It sounds pretty simple, doesn't it? And it is, when you know what you are doing.

To avoid any unpleasant surprises I always scheduled myself for a complete physical examination with my personal physician, Dr Strauss, before going in for my FAA and company exams. Shortly after turning fifty I complained to him that I had trouble sleeping on those Tokyo layovers, and felt very tired after one of those trips. We talked about my routine for a few minutes, then he asked me to review a recent trip and count how many cups of coffee I drank that day. I counted fourteen cups! Then he asked; "Why don't you have a soda water, or a tonic water instead of that automatic cup of coffee?" I never had any more trouble.

STORM CLOUDS

Late in 1968 the unthinkable happened; Juan Trippe retired.

I suspect that he felt that after 40 years at the helm, (if not always completely in charge) his work was done, and it was a good time to leave. The dream he and Bill Allen had was about to materialize in the form of the magnificent Boeing 747. Pan American Airways was in strong financial shape, with all divisions doing well, and its future was bright.

Harold Gray was his chosen successor, and had been groomed for years to step into the job. The employees—especially the aircrews—felt comfortable with the choice, as many of us had known Harold for a very long time. When Captain Edwin Musick was killed in a Sikorsky S-42 crash, Harold Gray inherited the mantle of the "Worlds Greatest Airline Pilot", and it fitted him well. He was a true pioneer in the art of oceanic flying, and had been very instrumental in developing the navigation techniques as well as the operating procedures on the flying boats. Now, many years later, he assumed a new command as the CEO of the world's greatest airline.

A short time before his unexpected decision to retire, Trippe had hired a new Vice-President; Najeeb Halaby, who had been a Navy test pilot, former head of the Federal Aviation Authority, and was a very warm "people-type" public figure. Although an outsider, he was named No. 2 to Gray in the new administration. His particular realm of authority was never defined, but as Halaby was a democrat and knew President Kennedy well, we supposed it would have something to do with Washington, D.C. As a public person Gray was something of a cold fish, public relations being one of the few things he did not do well. Halaby filled that gap admirably, and as President of the airline added a touch of warmth to the public perception.

Gray held the control wheel steady for a while, and then seemed to disappear. Rumors were soon confirmed that he was dying of cancer, and that was soon followed by his departure. The Board of Directors sadly accepted his resignation and turned the job over to Halaby. Captain Harold Gray died about a year later.

As the new CEO, "Jeeb" Halaby was an active, highly visible administrator. He loved airplanes, and personally test flew the fledgling 747 aircraft. He liked to sit in the jump seat on the aircraft and talk airplanes with the crew, and carry a pot of coffee from the galley. One evening he showed up, unannounced, at the San Francisco maintenance hangar and spent an hour talking with the mechanics about their problems. He was our kind of guy. He really seemed to be one of us, and we were hopeful that he would be able to get what he called "our airline" back on track.

The world economy plunged into a recession in 1969 and airline revenues were hard hit. The introduction of the 747 in January 1970 was not a smashing financial success as the industry was wallowing in over-capacity. Losses rapidly mounted and the recession wore on for two more years.

Upper management people in the PanAm building in New York did not share the employee's support of Halaby. He was not one of them, and was left to walk alone, in a sense. That is still my memory of Najeeb Halaby; walking alone. The Board of Directors, with Charles Lindbergh voting against him, soon showed Jeeb the exit door.

Next up was William Seawell, another outsider. Former Commanding General of the Strategic Air Command and Commandant of the Air Force Academy, he had a reputation as a no-nonsense administrator. After leaving military service he had worked briefly at American Airlines and at Rolls-Royce before he was recruited to be the President of PAA under Halaby. He soon established his rules in the Ivory Tower, and the lower levels as well. I heard that If you openly disagreed with him you were immediately sacked, and that those who survived did so with a zipped lip in his presence. Generally the cockpit opinion was that there was a lot of dead wood that needed clearing, and this guy might do a good job.

My eye-opener came one morning in Auckland, New Zealand. After a comfortable two-day layover at the Sheraton Hotel, I was preparing for a morning departure on the non-stop flight to Los Angeles. I woke early, showered and shaved, and put on my freshly cleaned uniform. I boarded the elevator and pushed the button for the lobby while deciding what I would order for breakfast. When the elevator stopped at the next floor I was delighted to see Mr. and Mrs. Seawell waiting. As they stepped in I said;

"Good Morning, Mr. and Mrs. Seawell"

He didn't even glance at me. He and his wife stepped in, turned around, and he jabbed a finger at the already illuminated "Lobby" button. Then they stood, staring straight ahead. As the elevator reached the lobby floor Mrs. Seawell looked over her shoulder at me and gave me a thin smile. He took her arm and they strode through the lobby and down the steps to a waiting limousine, then stood as the doorman rushed to open the Limo door for them. Then they were gone.

Had it been Juan Trippe he would have given me a gentle smile and nodded.

Had it been Harold Gray he would have said hello, and would probably have remembered my name.

Had it been Najeeb Halaby he would have shook my hand and said something cheerful.

Now I knew. With General William Seawell you did not have a name, or a face. You were just one of the necessary cogs in the machinery that made an airline function. This whole Pan American thing was about HIM, and no one else. It left me with a very uneasy feeling about the future of the airline.

Between 1972 and 1978, one third of the PAA employees were laid off as the company fought to stay afloat. At the end of that period airline revenues started to improve and the company made a modest profit for a couple of years.

During the Carter administration the airlines were deregulated, and the Civil Aeronautics Board, PanAm's nemesis for many years, was disbanded. Suddenly, any American airline could fly any domestic route it wanted, and charge whatever fare it fancied. It opened the door for all manner of start-up operators to pick a route and open an airline.

In the cockpits we talked about the possibilities. The company would be able to tie all of the coastal terminals together with a network of domestic routes. It was a golden opportunity to build a solid money making business, and the employees who had been furloughed could be recalled.

But it was not to be. From somewhere out in left field, General Seawell came up with the idea of buying National Airlines. National Airlines was one of the domestic trunk airlines serving the eastern United States and had a transcontinental route across the southern states. To the employees of both airlines it was difficult to find anything attractive about the purchase. A bidding war soon began against Texas International and Eastern airlines and the stock price of National Airlines doubled. Doubts about the wisdom of the deal were widely expressed in the newspapers, privately voiced in the office corridors of the airline, and openly cursed on the flight decks of both airlines. The Pan American Board of Directors had no public opinion, and no one at management level wanted to brave the wrath of the General by speaking out against the purchase. Our leader was firm and won the bidding battle, but he lost the war, as the cost was astronomical. To sell the deal he guaranteed every job at National. He promised to raise the National pay scales to at least equal PanAm's. And he sold out our furloughed pilots.

By the time the dust settled, and the Blue Ball crews of PanAm and the Orange Ball Crews of National had merged, we knew the end was in sight. Operating costs soared as the company tried to maintain too many different kinds of airplanes. There were no efficiencies of scale, as nobody at National could be eliminated. The bloated resulting airline was leaking money at every seam, while revenues were decreasing. Knowledgeable analysts said that Seawell's folly had cost the airline a billion dollars, and the bleeding was continuing.

The only way to keep the company afloat was to start selling the family jewels, one by one. The first to go were the Intercontinental Hotels, then the PanAm building, and finally the Pacific route system.

The cockpit conversations began to take a grim turn. The juniors talked about trying some other line of work. Senior people, like myself, were scratching down numbers from their pension statements, while the optimists were sure that things would improve. All of us agreed that Seawell had missed his chance to be a hero, and would go down in company history as a goat. He took what was kindly referred to as early retirement in 1978.

In retrospect the purchase of National Airlines made no economic sense. With deregulation Pan American could have opened any domestic route it wanted. The merged airline had three different wide-bodied aircraft, the Boeing 747, Douglas DC-10, and Lockheed 1011, each with a different engine manufacturer. This was clearly economic suicide.

HOPE PARKINSON KEWIN

1922-1976

In 1975 the Doctors found that Hope had cancer. It had started as breast cancer, but quickly spread insidiously through her body. I immediately resigned my office job, and flew a minimum schedule so as to be home as much as possible. Because the cancer was so far advanced when discovered, the doctors could not do anything to stop it. We tried some other treatments, like the controversial Laetrile, and started on a vegetarian juice diet. Nothing seemed to help, and she was rapidly failing. With her fate clearly known, Hope was remarkable. She was up and dressed every morning, wearing her usual smile and the daily routine was not changed. Above all, she wanted to show our sons that dying was a part of living.

And then she was gone. Our oldest son was at Graduate School in Boston, and because Hope went so quickly could not make it home in time. The two younger boys were with me at her side as she drifted off to a long sleep. And then I had to go tell Hope's mother that her youngest daughter had died.

A few days later the Chief Pilot called to offer his sympathies. He said that he had removed me from flight status indefinitely, and that I should call him when I wanted to go back to work.

I stared at the walls for a few weeks. When the world finally came back into focus I picked up the pieces and went back to work. I didn't know what else to do.

PHYLLIS

For five long years I filled my time with my job, repairs on the home, and some gold mining in the summer at my property in Northern California. My spare time in winter was spent rebuilding an old de Havilland "Tiger Moth" in my garage. Then I met Phyllis . . . . and life started again. We married in 1981, and she immediately got a dose of airline life as we set off for a two-week Tahiti Honeymoon on an employee discount ticket. We got the last two seats on the airplane. All of my friends and my sons embraced Phyllis, and her two daughters seemed to approve of me, so we quickly settled into a comfortable family routine. Phyllis continued to work for another year at her job as the Business Manager of an automobile dealership and then retired. Our plan was for her to retire after a year, and join me on some of my trips to places she had never seen, but the declining fortunes of the airline brought a change in our plans. In November, 1982, the company announced that another furlough was planned.

Several hundred pilots would have to be laid off indefinitely because of continuing losses, and schedule reductions. Because the furloughed pilots were eligible for "severance pay", and the layoffs would cause considerable training expense as job assignments were shuffled, the company decided to offer a sweetened package to any engineers who would opt for an early retirement. It was good enough that I couldn't say no, so on very short notice I retired, and December, 1982 was my last month of service.

Traditionally your last trip was something special in that you were allowed to bring your immediate family along. Fitch Robertson and I selected a "Double London" as our last trip, and Captain Mike Oliver also made that his choice. My wife Phyllis, and sons George, Jack, and Paul joined me. Fitch had his wife and three daughters, and Mike had his wife and two daughters so it was a built-in party! The families enjoyed the sights of pre-Christmas London, and the hospitality of some of my English cousins. They shopped, toured Windsor Castle, saw some shows, and had a grand time while Mike, Fitch and I flew to Los Angeles and back to London. On the last departure the three of us walked into the dispatch office with eleven sublo (subject to load) passengers on our minds, our families. Pre Christmas travel is always heavy, and the dispatcher cheerfully told us that we would have 3,000 pounds of extra fuel, but wouldn't be able to carry any sublo passengers. Captain Oliver explained that the three of us were on our last trip, with eleven sublos downstairs, and that there would not be any extra fuel, and that he would not close the doors until all of our families were on board. It only took a minute for this to sink in, and then everyone in the dispatch office came to shake our hands and cheer us on. I stood at the airplane entry door and counted noses, and personally closed the door. We made an on-time arrival at San Francisco where many friends came to help us celebrate.

Since my retirement in 1983 it has been painful to watch the downward spiral and disappearance of the company. The tragedy at Lockerbie was the final blow.

More than twenty years of retirement have dimmed some of the memories, but the mental efforts involved in writing these notes have done a good job of reviving many of them.

At three am it is amazing how the memories float up in your mind. Forty years and 31,000 hours, from the China Clipper to the Jumbo.

It was a wonderful ride.

Pan American Airways died in 1991. The bones have been picked over, and a few tries have been made to trade on the name, none of them successful.

Many of the tens of thousands of former employees cling to some memories through a variety of social organizations such as World Wings, Clipper Pioneers, Pan Am Historical Foundation, and local retiree groups. These groups not only help us keep connected with old friends, but also help keep alive the memory of a great airline, and that wisp of glory that was once our own Camelot.

FINAL NOTE

Recently some research was done by the "Canadian Military Flight Engineers" newsletter editor, Bruce Dyer, to determine who was the worlds first Flight Engineer. The result is very interesting.

In 1908 the Wright brothers had a chance for financial success with contracts from the U.S. government and a European consortium to produce an airplane capable of carrying two people 125 miles at a speed of 40 miles per hour. Time was limited, but with Charles Taylor's help they produced a new 40 horsepower engine and modified the "Wright Flyer 3" airplane with a second seat.

Charley Furnas had served four years as a "Mechanic's Mate" in the U.S. Navy, and after discharge found part time work with the brothers. The early tests of the new engine showed it would easily overheat under full power, but the flight tests could not wait for alterations. Charley Furnas flew as the second crewmember on all of the early test flights of the new airplane. His job was to operate and monitor the engine.

Charley Furnas was the first airplane passenger as well as the first Flight Engineer. Who will be the last?

BVG